Media Manipulation

Decoding the Influence of Fake News and Propaganda

Simon Elliott

The presentation of the information is without contract or any type of guarantee assurance. The trademarks that are used are without any consent, and the publication of the trademark is without permission or backing by the trademark owner. All trademarks and brands within this book are for clarifying purposes only and are the owned by the owners themselves, not affiliated with this document.

Table of Contents

chapter 1

Introduction to Media Manipulation

The Evolution of Media From Print to Digital

The journey of media from print to digital is a fascinating tale of transformation, innovation, and adaptation. It begins in the 15th century with the invention of the printing press by Johannes Gutenberg, a pivotal moment that revolutionized the way information was disseminated. Before this invention, books were laboriously hand-copied, making them scarce and expensive. The printing press democratized knowledge, allowing for the mass production of books and pamphlets, which in turn fueled the spread of ideas and literacy. This era marked the beginning of print media, which would dominate the landscape for centuries.

As print media evolved, newspapers emerged as a powerful force in the 17th century. They became the primary source of news and information, shaping public opinion and holding power to account. The rise of newspapers coincided with the Age of Enlightenment, a period characterized by intellectual and cultural growth. Newspapers played a crucial role in this era, providing a platform for debate and discussion. They were instrumental in the dissemination of revolutionary ideas, contributing to significant historical events such as the American and French Revolutions.

The 19th century saw further advancements in print media with the introduction of magazines and periodicals. These publications catered to a wide range of interests, from politics and science to fashion and entertainment. The diversity of content available in magazines expanded the reach of print media, appealing to a broader audience. The industrial revolution brought technological innovations such as the steam-powered printing press, which increased the speed and efficiency of production, further solidifying the dominance of print media.

The 20th century ushered in the age of broadcast media, with the advent of radio and television. These new forms of media offered a dynamic and immediate way to reach audiences, challenging the supremacy of print. Radio became a household staple, providing news, entertainment, and music to listeners around the world. It played a significant role during World War II, serving as a tool for propaganda and morale-boosting broadcasts. Television followed, captivating audiences with its visual storytelling capabilities. The introduction of color television in the 1960s further enhanced its appeal, making it a dominant force in the media landscape.

Despite the rise of broadcast media, print continued to thrive, adapting to the changing times. Newspapers and magazines embraced new printing technologies and design innovations to remain relevant. However, the seeds of change were already sown, as the digital revolution loomed on the horizon. The late 20th century witnessed the birth of the internet, a technological marvel that would forever alter the media landscape.

The transition from print to digital media was not instantaneous but rather a gradual process marked by experimentation and adaptation. The internet offered unprecedented opportunities for content creation and distribution, challenging traditional media models. Online news websites emerged, providing real-time updates and interactive features that print could not match. The digital age also saw the rise of blogs and independent media outlets, giving voice to diverse perspectives and democratizing content creation.

Social media platforms further accelerated the shift to digital, transforming the way people consume and share information. Platforms like Facebook, Twitter, and Instagram became integral parts of daily life, offering users a personalized news feed and the ability to engage with content in real-time. The viral nature of social media allowed for the rapid spread of information, both accurate and misleading, highlighting the need for media literacy in the digital age.

The evolution from print to digital has not been without its challenges. Traditional media organizations have had to adapt to survive in an increasingly digital world. Many newspapers and magazines have transitioned to online formats, offering digital subscriptions and leveraging multimedia content to engage audiences. The decline of print advertising revenue has forced media companies to explore new business models, such as paywalls and sponsored content, to sustain their operations.

The digital age has also raised important questions about the quality and credibility of information. The ease of publishing online has led to an explosion of content, making it difficult for audiences to discern reliable sources from misinformation. This has underscored the importance of critical thinking and media literacy, as individuals navigate the vast digital landscape.

Despite these challenges, the digital revolution has brought about significant benefits. It has democratized access to information, allowing people from all corners of the globe to connect and share ideas. The interactive nature of digital media has fostered greater engagement and participation, empowering individuals to become active contributors to the media ecosystem.

The evolution of media from print to digital is a testament to the resilience and adaptability of the industry. It reflects the ever-changing nature of technology and society, as media continues to evolve to meet the needs and preferences of audiences. As we look to the future, the media landscape will undoubtedly continue to transform, driven by advancements in technology and shifts in consumer behavior.

Defining Fake News and Propaganda

In the labyrinth of modern media, the terms "fake news" and "propaganda" have become ubiquitous, yet their meanings often remain elusive. To navigate this complex terrain, it's essential to dissect these concepts, understanding their origins, characteristics, and implications. Fake news, a term that has gained prominence in recent years, refers to false or misleading information presented as news. Its purpose is often to deceive, manipulate, or influence public perception. Unlike satire or parody, which are intended for entertainment, fake news is crafted with the intent to mislead.

The roots of fake news can be traced back to the early days of print media, where sensationalism and yellow journalism were rampant. However, the digital age has amplified its reach and impact, allowing misinformation to spread rapidly across the globe. The internet and social media platforms have become fertile ground for fake news, where it can be disseminated with ease and reach millions within moments. This proliferation has been fueled by the low barriers to entry for content creation and the viral nature of digital platforms.

Fake news often thrives on sensationalism, exploiting emotions such as fear, anger, or outrage to capture attention. It frequently employs clickbait headlines, designed to entice users to click and share without verifying the content's accuracy. The spread of fake news is further exacerbated by confirmation bias, where individuals are more likely to believe and share information that aligns with their pre-existing beliefs or opinions. This creates echo chambers, where misinformation is reinforced and amplified within like-minded communities.

Propaganda, on the other hand, is a more established concept with a long history. It refers to the systematic dissemination of information, ideas, or rumors to influence public opinion or behavior. Unlike fake news, which is often created by individuals or small groups, propaganda is typically orchestrated by governments, political parties, or organizations with specific agendas. Its purpose is to shape perceptions, control narratives, and achieve strategic objectives.

The use of propaganda dates back to ancient civilizations, where rulers employed various means to control and influence their subjects. In the modern era, propaganda became a powerful tool during times of war and political upheaval. The 20th century witnessed the rise of state-sponsored propaganda, with regimes using mass media to promote ideologies and suppress dissent. Propaganda techniques have evolved over time, adapting to new technologies and media landscapes.

One of the key characteristics of propaganda is its reliance on emotional appeals. It often uses symbols, slogans, and imagery to evoke strong emotional responses, bypassing rational analysis. Propaganda may also employ selective presentation of facts, omitting or distorting information to fit a particular narrative. This manipulation of information can create a skewed perception of reality, influencing public attitudes and behaviors.

In the digital age, the lines between fake news and propaganda have become increasingly blurred. Both exploit the same platforms and techniques to achieve their goals, making it challenging to distinguish between them. The rise of social media has democratized content creation, allowing anyone with an internet connection to produce and share information. This has led to an explosion of content, where fake news and propaganda can easily blend into the noise.

The impact of fake news and propaganda on society is profound. They can undermine trust in media and institutions, polarize communities, and influence political outcomes. The spread of misinformation can have real-world consequences, from inciting violence to affecting public health and safety. In an era where information is abundant, the ability to critically evaluate and discern credible sources is more important than ever.

To combat the influence of fake news and propaganda, media literacy is crucial. Individuals must be equipped with the skills to critically assess information, identify biases, and verify sources. This involves questioning the credibility of the content, examining the motives behind it, and cross-referencing with reliable sources. Media literacy education can empower individuals to navigate the complex media landscape, making informed decisions and resisting manipulation.

Efforts to address fake news and propaganda also require collaboration between governments, media organizations, and technology companies. Regulatory frameworks can be established to hold platforms accountable for the spread of misinformation, while media organizations can uphold journalistic standards and ethics. Technology companies can develop algorithms and tools to detect and flag false information, reducing its visibility and reach.

Ultimately, the battle against fake news and propaganda is a collective responsibility. It requires vigilance, critical thinking, and a commitment to truth and transparency. As consumers of information, individuals have the power to shape the media landscape by demanding accuracy, accountability, and integrity. By fostering a culture of media literacy and critical inquiry, society can build resilience against the forces of misinformation and manipulation.

Historical Context Propaganda Through the Ages

Throughout history, propaganda has been a powerful tool wielded by those in positions of authority to shape public perception and influence societal behavior. Its roots stretch back to ancient civilizations, where leaders recognized the potential of persuasive communication to consolidate power and control narratives. By examining the evolution of propaganda across different eras, we can gain insight into its enduring impact and the ways it has been adapted to suit the needs of various regimes and movements.

In ancient times, propaganda was often intertwined with religion and mythology. Rulers and priests used religious texts, symbols, and rituals to legitimize their authority and reinforce social hierarchies. The construction of monumental architecture, such as temples and pyramids, served as a testament to the divine right of kings and the power of the state. These structures were not only physical manifestations of power but also tools of propaganda, conveying messages of stability, continuity, and divine favor.

The Roman Empire provides a compelling example of early propaganda techniques. Emperors employed a range of methods to project their image and promote their policies. Coins bearing the likeness of the emperor circulated throughout the empire, serving as a constant reminder of imperial authority. Public spectacles, such as gladiatorial games and triumphal processions, were orchestrated to celebrate military victories and reinforce the emperor's role as a protector of the people. The use of inscriptions and monuments further solidified the emperor's legacy, ensuring that his achievements were immortalized in stone.

As societies evolved, so too did the methods of propaganda. The invention of the printing press in the 15th century revolutionized the dissemination of information, making it possible to reach a wider audience with greater efficiency. This technological advancement played a crucial role in the spread of propaganda during the Reformation and the subsequent religious conflicts in Europe. Both Protestant and Catholic factions utilized pamphlets, broadsheets, and woodcuts to promote their respective doctrines and vilify their opponents. The power of the printed word became evident as propaganda fueled religious fervor and intensified sectarian divisions.

The 20th century marked a turning point in the history of propaganda, as it became an integral component of modern warfare and political strategy. During World War I, governments recognized the importance of controlling information and shaping public opinion to maintain morale and support for the war effort. Propaganda agencies were established to produce posters, films, and other media that glorified the nation's cause and demonized the enemy. The use of propaganda extended beyond the battlefield, influencing civilian populations and fostering a sense of national unity.

The interwar period saw the rise of totalitarian regimes that harnessed propaganda to consolidate power and suppress dissent. In Nazi Germany, propaganda was elevated to an art form under the direction of Joseph Goebbels, the Minister of Propaganda. The regime employed a sophisticated array of techniques, including films, radio broadcasts, and mass rallies, to indoctrinate the populace and promote the ideals of the Third Reich. The manipulation of information and the creation of a cult of personality around Adolf Hitler exemplified the potential of propaganda to control and mobilize entire societies.

Similarly, the Soviet Union under Joseph Stalin utilized propaganda to maintain control over the population and promote the ideals of communism. The state-controlled media portrayed Stalin as a benevolent leader and the embodiment of the people's will. Art, literature, and music were co-opted to serve the interests of the regime, glorifying the achievements of the Soviet state and vilifying its enemies. The use of propaganda extended to education, where curricula were designed to instill loyalty to the party and adherence to its ideology.

The Cold War era witnessed a global propaganda battle between the United States and the Soviet Union, as both superpowers sought to win hearts and minds in the struggle for ideological supremacy. The United States employed a range of strategies, including cultural diplomacy, international broadcasting, and covert operations, to promote the values of democracy and capitalism. The Soviet Union countered with its own propaganda campaigns, emphasizing the virtues of socialism and the failures of Western imperialism. This ideological contest played out on a global stage, influencing political movements and shaping the course of history.

In the contemporary era, the advent of digital technology and the internet has transformed the landscape of propaganda once again. The rise of social media platforms has democratized the production and dissemination of information, allowing individuals and organizations to reach vast audiences with unprecedented speed and efficiency. This has created new opportunities for propaganda, as well as new challenges in discerning truth from manipulation. The digital age has blurred the lines between propaganda, advertising, and entertainment, making it increasingly difficult to identify and counteract its influence.

Despite the changes in technology and media, the fundamental principles of propaganda remain consistent. It relies on emotional appeals, repetition, and the manipulation of information to achieve its objectives. Propaganda seeks to simplify complex issues, create scapegoats, and foster a sense of belonging or fear. It thrives in environments where critical thinking is suppressed, and dissenting voices are marginalized.

The Role of Media in Society

Media has long been a cornerstone of society, serving as a conduit for information, a platform for discourse, and a mirror reflecting the cultural zeitgeist. Its role has evolved alongside technological advancements, shaping and being shaped by the societies it serves. From the earliest forms of communication to the digital age, media has been instrumental in influencing public opinion, driving social change, and fostering a sense of community.

In its earliest incarnations, media took the form of oral traditions and storytelling, where bards and griots passed down knowledge, history, and cultural values through generations. These narratives were not only a means of preserving heritage but also a way to instill moral lessons and societal norms. As societies developed written language, the role of media expanded to include manuscripts and texts, which allowed for the dissemination of ideas across greater distances and to a broader audience.

The invention of the printing press in the 15th century marked a significant turning point in the history of media. It democratized access to information, enabling the mass production of books, pamphlets, and newspapers. This technological breakthrough facilitated the spread of revolutionary ideas, such as those of the Enlightenment and the Reformation, challenging established authorities and sparking intellectual and social movements. The printed word became a powerful tool for education and empowerment, laying the groundwork for the modern media landscape.

As the centuries progressed, the advent of radio and television further transformed the role of media in society. These new mediums brought information and entertainment directly into people's homes, creating a shared cultural experience and a sense of immediacy. Radio broadcasts provided real-time updates on world events, while television introduced visual storytelling that captivated audiences and shaped public perceptions. The reach and influence of these mediums were unparalleled, as they became integral to daily life and a primary source of news and entertainment.

The rise of the internet and digital media in the late 20th century revolutionized the way information is produced, consumed, and shared. The internet has broken down geographical barriers, allowing for the instantaneous exchange of information across the globe. Social media platforms have given individuals a voice, enabling them to participate in public discourse and connect with like-minded communities. This democratization of media has empowered citizens to hold institutions accountable and advocate for social change, as seen in movements such as the Arab Spring and #MeToo.

Despite its many benefits, the digital age has also introduced new challenges and complexities. The sheer volume of information available online can be overwhelming, making it difficult for individuals to discern credible sources from misinformation. The rise of echo chambers and filter bubbles has contributed to the polarization of public opinion, as algorithms curate content that reinforces existing beliefs and biases. The spread of fake news and disinformation campaigns has further eroded trust in media institutions, highlighting the need for media literacy and critical thinking skills.

Media's role in shaping public opinion cannot be overstated. It serves as a gatekeeper, determining which stories are told and how they are framed. The language and imagery used in media coverage can influence perceptions and attitudes, often reinforcing stereotypes or perpetuating biases. For example, the portrayal of marginalized communities in news and entertainment media can impact societal attitudes and contribute to systemic inequalities. As such, media has a responsibility to provide balanced and accurate reporting, ensuring diverse voices and perspectives are represented.

In addition to informing and influencing public opinion, media plays a crucial role in fostering social cohesion and cultural identity. It provides a platform for shared experiences, whether through national events, popular television shows, or viral internet trends. Media can bring people together, creating a sense of belonging and community. It also serves as a cultural archive, preserving and documenting the stories, art, and achievements of a society for future generations.

The economic impact of media is another important aspect to consider. The media industry is a significant driver of economic growth, providing jobs and generating revenue through advertising, subscriptions, and content production. It also plays a role in shaping consumer behavior, as advertising and marketing campaigns influence purchasing decisions and trends. The relationship between media and commerce is symbiotic, with each influencing and benefiting from the other.

As media continues to evolve, its role in society will undoubtedly change. Emerging technologies, such as virtual reality and artificial intelligence, are poised to transform the media landscape once again, offering new possibilities for storytelling and audience engagement. However, the core functions of media—to inform, entertain, and connect—will remain constant. The challenge lies in navigating the complexities of the digital age while upholding the principles of accuracy, fairness, and inclusivity.

To ensure media fulfills its role effectively, it is essential to promote media literacy and critical thinking skills among the public. Individuals must be equipped to evaluate sources, recognize biases, and engage with diverse perspectives. Media organizations, too, have a responsibility to uphold ethical standards and prioritize transparency and accountability. By fostering a media-literate society and holding media institutions to high standards, we can harness the power of media to drive positive change and strengthen the fabric of society.

The Impact of Media Manipulation on Public Perception

Media manipulation has become an increasingly pervasive force in shaping public perception, often blurring the lines between reality and fiction. This phenomenon, driven by various actors with diverse agendas, has profound implications for how individuals understand and engage with the world around them. The subtle art of media manipulation involves the strategic presentation of information, often with the intent to influence opinions, behaviors, or beliefs. As media consumers, it is crucial to recognize these tactics and develop the skills necessary to navigate the complex landscape of modern media.

One of the most common forms of media manipulation is the selective presentation of information. By emphasizing certain facts while omitting others, media outlets can craft narratives that align with specific agendas. This selective reporting can create a skewed perception of events, leading audiences to form opinions based on incomplete or biased information. For instance, the portrayal of political candidates during election cycles often highlights particular aspects of their platforms or personal lives, shaping voter perceptions and potentially influencing electoral outcomes.

Framing is another powerful tool used in media manipulation. The way a story is presented—through language, imagery, and context—can significantly impact how it is perceived by the audience. By framing an issue in a particular light, media can evoke specific emotions or reactions, guiding public discourse in a desired direction. Consider the coverage of social issues such as immigration or climate change; the choice of words and images can evoke empathy, fear, or urgency, shaping public attitudes and policy debates.

The rise of digital media has amplified the potential for media manipulation, as information can be disseminated rapidly and widely with minimal oversight. Social media platforms, in particular, have become fertile ground for the spread of manipulated content, as algorithms prioritize engagement over accuracy. This environment allows for the proliferation of misinformation and disinformation, which can be weaponized to sow discord, polarize communities, or undermine trust in institutions.

Misinformation refers to false or misleading information shared without malicious intent, while disinformation is deliberately crafted to deceive or mislead. Both forms of manipulated content can have significant consequences, as they contribute to the erosion of trust in media and institutions. The spread of false information can lead to confusion, fear, and division, as individuals struggle to discern fact from fiction in an increasingly complex media landscape.

The impact of media manipulation extends beyond individual perceptions, influencing societal norms and values. By shaping the narratives that dominate public discourse, media can reinforce stereotypes, perpetuate biases, and marginalize certain groups. This can have lasting effects on social cohesion and equality, as marginalized communities may struggle to have their voices heard and their experiences validated.

To counteract the effects of media manipulation, it is essential to cultivate media literacy skills. Media literacy involves the ability to critically analyze and evaluate media content, recognizing biases, agendas, and manipulation tactics. By developing these skills, individuals can become more discerning consumers of information, better equipped to navigate the complexities of the media landscape.

One practical approach to enhancing media literacy is to diversify the sources of information consumed. By seeking out multiple perspectives and engaging with a variety of media outlets, individuals can gain a more comprehensive understanding of issues and events. This practice encourages critical thinking and helps to identify potential biases or omissions in reporting.

Fact-checking is another crucial component of media literacy. Before accepting information as truth, it is important to verify its accuracy through reputable sources. Fact-checking organizations and tools can assist in this process, providing evidence-based assessments of claims and helping to debunk false information.

Engaging in open dialogue and discussion with others can also help to counteract media manipulation. By sharing diverse perspectives and challenging assumptions, individuals can foster a more nuanced understanding of complex issues. This collaborative approach encourages empathy and understanding, bridging divides and promoting social cohesion.

Media organizations, too, have a responsibility to uphold ethical standards and prioritize transparency and accountability. By adhering to principles of accuracy, fairness, and inclusivity, media can work to rebuild trust with audiences and mitigate the effects of manipulation. This includes providing context for stories, acknowledging biases, and correcting errors promptly.

The role of education in combating media manipulation cannot be overstated. By incorporating media literacy into educational curricula, schools can equip students with the skills necessary to navigate the media landscape critically and responsibly. This foundational knowledge empowers individuals to engage with media thoughtfully, fostering informed and active citizenship.

As media continues to evolve, the tactics and techniques of manipulation will undoubtedly adapt. Emerging technologies, such as deepfakes and synthetic media, present new challenges and opportunities for manipulation. These advancements underscore the importance of remaining vigilant and informed, as the line between reality and fiction becomes increasingly blurred.

Chapter 2

The Mechanics of Fake News

Identifying Fake News
Key Characteristics

In the digital age, the proliferation of information has made it increasingly challenging to discern fact from fiction. The rise of fake news, a term that has become synonymous with misinformation and disinformation, poses a significant threat to informed decision-making and public discourse. Understanding the key characteristics of fake news is essential for individuals seeking to navigate the complex media landscape and protect themselves from deception.

Fake news often thrives on sensationalism, capturing attention with eye-catching headlines and dramatic narratives. These stories are designed to evoke strong emotional reactions, such as anger, fear, or outrage, prompting readers to share the content without verifying its accuracy. Sensational headlines may include exaggerated claims or misleading language, creating a sense of urgency that encourages impulsive sharing. By recognizing this tactic, individuals can pause and critically evaluate the content before accepting it as truth.

Another hallmark of fake news is the lack of credible sources or evidence to support its claims. Legitimate news articles typically cite reputable sources, providing context and evidence to substantiate their reporting. In contrast, fake news often relies on anonymous or unverified sources, making it difficult to trace the origin of the information. When encountering a news story, it is important to scrutinize the sources cited and assess their credibility. If the article lacks verifiable evidence or relies on dubious sources, it may be a red flag indicating the presence of fake news.

The use of manipulated images or videos is a common tactic employed by purveyors of fake news. Visual content can be easily altered or taken out of context to support false narratives, making it a powerful tool for deception. For example, a photograph may be digitally edited to depict an event that never occurred, or a video clip may be selectively edited to misrepresent the actions or statements of individuals. To identify manipulated visuals, individuals can use reverse image search tools to trace the origin of an image or seek out the full context of a video.

Fake news often exploits confirmation bias, the tendency for individuals to favor information that aligns with their preexisting beliefs or opinions. By presenting content that reinforces these beliefs, fake news can be particularly persuasive, as it validates the reader's worldview. This bias can lead individuals to accept false information without question, as it resonates with their personal perspectives. To counteract confirmation bias, it is important to approach news with an open mind and consider alternative viewpoints, even if they challenge one's beliefs.

The presence of grammatical errors, spelling mistakes, or awkward phrasing can also be indicative of fake news. While legitimate news organizations typically adhere to editorial standards and employ professional writers, fake news sites may lack such oversight, resulting in poorly written content. When evaluating a news article, attention to detail can reveal inconsistencies or errors that undermine its credibility. If an article is riddled with mistakes, it may be a sign that it was hastily produced without regard for accuracy.

The domain or URL of a website can provide clues about the legitimacy of the content it hosts. Fake news sites often mimic the appearance of reputable news organizations, using similar logos or website designs to deceive readers. However, a closer examination of the URL may reveal subtle differences, such as misspellings or unusual domain extensions. By verifying the authenticity of a website, individuals can avoid falling victim to fake news masquerading as legitimate journalism.

The motivations behind fake news can vary, ranging from financial gain to political influence. Some fake news sites generate revenue through advertising, capitalizing on high traffic volumes driven by sensational content. Others may seek to sway public opinion or undermine trust in institutions by spreading false information. Understanding the potential motivations behind fake news can provide insight into its purpose and help individuals assess its credibility.

To combat the spread of fake news, individuals can take proactive steps to verify the information they encounter. Fact-checking organizations and tools offer valuable resources for assessing the accuracy of claims and debunking false information. By consulting these sources, individuals can make informed decisions about the credibility of a news story.

Engaging in critical thinking and skepticism is essential when evaluating news content. Rather than accepting information at face value, individuals should question the validity of the claims and seek out additional sources to corroborate the story. This approach encourages a more nuanced understanding of complex issues and reduces the likelihood of falling victim to fake news.

Media literacy education plays a crucial role in equipping individuals with the skills necessary to identify fake news. By fostering critical thinking and analytical skills, media literacy programs empower individuals to navigate the media landscape with confidence and discernment. Educational initiatives can help individuals recognize the tactics used by fake news and develop strategies for verifying information.

The responsibility to combat fake news extends beyond individual media consumers to include media organizations and platforms. By prioritizing accuracy and transparency, media outlets can rebuild trust with audiences and mitigate the effects of misinformation. Social media platforms, in particular, have a role to play in curbing the spread of fake news by implementing measures to identify and flag false content.

As the digital landscape continues to evolve, the tactics and techniques of fake news will undoubtedly adapt. Emerging technologies, such as deepfakes and synthetic media, present new challenges for identifying and combating fake news. These advancements underscore the importance of remaining vigilant and informed, as the line between reality and fiction becomes increasingly blurred.

The Psychology Behind Believing Fake News

The human mind is a complex and fascinating entity, capable of remarkable feats of reasoning and creativity. Yet, it is also susceptible to biases and cognitive shortcuts that can lead to the acceptance of false information. Understanding the psychology behind why people believe fake news is crucial for developing strategies to combat its spread and mitigate its impact on society.

One of the primary psychological factors contributing to the belief in fake news is confirmation bias. This cognitive bias leads individuals to favor information that aligns with their preexisting beliefs and dismiss information that contradicts them. When people encounter news stories that reinforce their worldview, they are more likely to accept them as true, even if the stories are false. This bias is particularly potent in the context of fake news, as it exploits individuals' desire for validation and certainty. By recognizing the influence of confirmation bias, individuals can become more aware of their own cognitive tendencies and approach news with a more critical mindset.

The phenomenon of cognitive dissonance also plays a significant role in the acceptance of fake news. Cognitive dissonance occurs when individuals experience discomfort due to holding conflicting beliefs or attitudes. To alleviate this discomfort, people may rationalize or justify their beliefs, even in the face of contradictory evidence. Fake news can serve as a tool for resolving cognitive dissonance by providing information that supports an individual's existing beliefs, thereby reducing the tension between conflicting ideas. Understanding this psychological mechanism can help individuals recognize when they are prioritizing comfort over truth and encourage them to seek out diverse perspectives.

The role of social identity in shaping beliefs cannot be underestimated. People often derive a sense of belonging and self-worth from their affiliation with social groups, such as political parties, religious communities, or cultural identities. These group affiliations can influence how individuals perceive and interpret information, as they are motivated to maintain a positive image of their group. Fake news that aligns with the values or beliefs of a particular group can be especially persuasive, as it reinforces group identity and cohesion. By acknowledging the impact of social identity on belief formation, individuals can become more mindful of how group dynamics may influence their acceptance of information.

The concept of the "illusory truth effect" further elucidates why people may believe fake news. This psychological phenomenon occurs when repeated exposure to a statement increases the likelihood of it being perceived as true, regardless of its accuracy. The more frequently individuals encounter a piece of information, the more familiar it becomes, leading to a sense of credibility. Fake news often capitalizes on this effect by circulating widely and repeatedly, creating an illusion of truth through sheer repetition. To counteract the illusory truth effect, individuals can actively seek out original sources and verify the accuracy of information before accepting it as fact.

Emotional appeal is another powerful tool used by fake news to capture attention and influence beliefs. Stories that evoke strong emotions, such as fear, anger, or empathy, are more likely to be remembered and shared. Emotional arousal can impair critical thinking and lead individuals to prioritize emotional responses over rational analysis. Fake news often exploits this vulnerability by crafting narratives that resonate emotionally with readers, making it difficult to separate fact from fiction. By cultivating emotional awareness, individuals can learn to recognize when their emotions are being manipulated and approach news with a more balanced perspective.

The role of cognitive load in processing information is also relevant to understanding why people believe fake news. Cognitive load refers to the mental effort required to process and understand information. When individuals are overwhelmed with information or distracted by other tasks, they may rely on cognitive shortcuts, such as heuristics, to make quick judgments. Fake news can take advantage of high cognitive load by presenting simple, easily digestible narratives that require minimal cognitive effort to process. By managing cognitive load and creating an environment conducive to thoughtful reflection, individuals can improve their ability to critically evaluate information.

The influence of authority figures and perceived expertise can also contribute to the belief in fake news. People often rely on trusted sources or experts to guide their understanding of complex issues. When fake news is endorsed by individuals perceived as authoritative or knowledgeable, it can lend credibility to false information. This reliance on authority can be particularly problematic when individuals lack the expertise to independently verify the accuracy of claims. By fostering critical thinking skills and encouraging skepticism, individuals can become more discerning consumers of information and less susceptible to the influence of perceived authority.

The psychological concept of "motivated reasoning" further explains why individuals may accept fake news. Motivated reasoning refers to the tendency for individuals to process information in a way that aligns with their desires or goals. When people are motivated to believe a particular narrative, they may selectively attend to information that supports their desired conclusion and dismiss information that contradicts it. Fake news can exploit motivated reasoning by presenting information that aligns with individuals' goals or aspirations, making it more likely to be accepted as true. By cultivating self-awareness and reflecting on personal motivations, individuals can become more objective in their evaluation of information.

The impact of social media and digital platforms on the spread of fake news cannot be overlooked. These platforms often prioritize engagement and virality, leading to the rapid dissemination of sensational or emotionally charged content. The algorithms that govern these platforms can create echo chambers, where individuals are exposed primarily to information that reinforces their beliefs. This environment can exacerbate the psychological factors that contribute to the belief in fake news, as individuals are less likely to encounter diverse perspectives or contradictory information. By actively seeking out diverse sources and engaging with a variety of viewpoints, individuals can break free from the confines of echo chambers and develop a more nuanced understanding of complex issues.

Case Studies Notorious Fake News Stories

In the vast landscape of information, certain fake news stories have managed to capture the public's attention, leaving a lasting impact on society. These notorious cases serve as cautionary tales, illustrating the power of misinformation and the importance of critical thinking. By examining these stories, we can gain insight into the mechanisms that allow fake news to thrive and the consequences it can have on individuals and communities.

One of the most infamous fake news stories in recent history is the "Pizzagate" conspiracy theory. This baseless claim emerged during the 2016 U.S. presidential election, alleging that a Washington, D.C. pizzeria was the center of a child trafficking ring linked to high-profile political figures. The story gained traction on social media platforms, fueled by a combination of confirmation bias and emotional appeal. Despite the lack of evidence, the narrative spread rapidly, culminating in a dangerous incident where an armed individual entered the pizzeria, seeking to "rescue" the alleged victims. This case highlights the potential for fake news to incite real-world actions, demonstrating the need for vigilance and skepticism when encountering sensational claims.

Another notable example is the false story surrounding the death of a young boy in the aftermath of Hurricane Katrina. In the chaotic days following the disaster, rumors circulated that a child had been brutally murdered in the New Orleans Superdome, where thousands of evacuees had sought refuge. This story, though entirely fabricated, was reported by several media outlets, contributing to a narrative of lawlessness and violence. The spread of this fake news exacerbated the already tense situation, influencing public perception and shaping the response to the crisis. The case underscores the responsibility of media organizations to verify information before publication, as well as the role of consumers in questioning the veracity of sensational reports.

The "War of the Worlds" radio broadcast in 1938 serves as a historical example of how fake news can exploit human psychology. Orson Welles' dramatization of H.G. Wells' novel was presented as a series of news bulletins, leading some listeners to believe that an actual Martian invasion was underway. The broadcast caused widespread panic, with people fleeing their homes and contacting authorities in fear. This incident illustrates the power of media to influence emotions and behavior, particularly when information is presented in a credible format. It also highlights the importance of media literacy, as individuals must be equipped to discern between fiction and reality in an increasingly complex information landscape.

The spread of fake news is not limited to the United States. In India, a series of false stories circulated on social media platforms, claiming that child kidnappers were operating in various regions. These rumors led to a wave of mob violence, resulting in the deaths of several innocent individuals. The rapid dissemination of these stories was facilitated by messaging apps, which allowed for the unchecked spread of misinformation. This case demonstrates the global nature of the fake news phenomenon and the urgent need for effective strategies to combat its spread. It also emphasizes the role of technology companies in addressing the challenges posed by misinformation on their platforms.

The "Birther" conspiracy theory, which questioned the legitimacy of President Barack Obama's birth certificate, is another example of a fake news story with significant political implications. Despite clear evidence to the contrary, the narrative persisted for years, fueled by partisan motivations and media coverage. This case highlights the intersection of fake news and political agendas, as well as the challenges of debunking persistent falsehoods. It also underscores the importance of transparency and accountability in public discourse, as misinformation can undermine trust in institutions and erode democratic processes.

The "Vaccines cause autism" myth is a particularly damaging example of fake news in the realm of public health. This false claim originated from a discredited study published in the late 1990s, which suggested a link between the MMR vaccine and autism. Despite being thoroughly debunked by the scientific community, the myth has persisted, contributing to vaccine hesitancy and outbreaks of preventable diseases. This case illustrates the long-lasting impact of fake news on public health and the importance of evidence-based communication. It also highlights the role of healthcare professionals and educators in countering misinformation and promoting informed decision-making.

The "Satanic Panic" of the 1980s and 1990s serves as a reminder of the power of moral panic to fuel fake news. During this period, a wave of false allegations emerged, claiming that satanic cults were engaging in ritual abuse and sacrificing children. These stories, often lacking credible evidence, were sensationalized by media outlets and led to numerous wrongful convictions. The case demonstrates how fear and hysteria can amplify fake news, resulting in significant harm to individuals and communities. It also underscores the need for critical thinking and due process in the face of sensational claims.

The "Death Panels" myth, which emerged during the debate over healthcare reform in the United States, is another example of fake news with policy implications. This false narrative claimed that proposed legislation would create panels to decide who would receive life-saving treatment, effectively rationing care. Despite being debunked, the myth persisted, influencing public opinion and shaping the policy debate. This case highlights the role of misinformation in shaping public policy and the importance of clear, accurate communication from policymakers and media outlets.

The "5G causes COVID-19" conspiracy theory is a recent example of fake news in the context of a global pandemic. This baseless claim suggested that the rollout of 5G technology was linked to the spread of the coronavirus, leading to acts of vandalism against telecommunications infrastructure. The rapid spread of this misinformation was facilitated by social media platforms, illustrating the challenges of combating fake news in a digital age. This case underscores the importance of timely, accurate information from trusted sources, as well as the need for collaboration between governments, technology companies, and civil society to address the spread of misinformation.

The Role of Algorithms in Spreading Misinformation

Algorithms, the invisible architects of our digital experiences, play a pivotal role in shaping the information we consume. These complex sets of rules and calculations determine what content appears in our social media feeds, search engine results, and even the advertisements we encounter online. While algorithms are designed to enhance user experience by personalizing content, they can inadvertently contribute to the spread of misinformation. Understanding how algorithms function and their impact on information dissemination is crucial in addressing the challenges posed by misinformation in the digital age.

At the heart of many algorithms is the goal of maximizing user engagement. Social media platforms, for instance, rely on algorithms to curate content that keeps users scrolling, clicking, and interacting. This is achieved by analyzing user behavior, such as likes, shares, and comments, to predict what content will capture their attention. However, this focus on engagement can create an environment where sensational or emotionally charged content is prioritized over factual information. Misinformation, often crafted to evoke strong emotional responses, can thrive in such an ecosystem, as it is more likely to be shared and spread rapidly.

The phenomenon of filter bubbles further illustrates the role of algorithms in spreading misinformation. As algorithms tailor content to individual preferences, users are often exposed to information that reinforces their existing beliefs and opinions. This creates an echo chamber effect, where diverse perspectives are limited, and misinformation can flourish unchecked. In these insular environments, false narratives can gain traction, as users are less likely to encounter content that challenges or debunks misleading claims. The result is a fragmented information landscape, where misinformation can persist and proliferate.

Search engines, too, are not immune to the influence of algorithms in spreading misinformation. The algorithms that power search engines are designed to deliver the most relevant results based on user queries. However, relevance is not synonymous with accuracy. In some cases, search algorithms may prioritize content that is popular or frequently linked, regardless of its veracity. This can lead to the amplification of misinformation, as false or misleading content may appear prominently in search results, lending it an air of credibility.

The role of algorithms in spreading misinformation is further complicated by the phenomenon of algorithmic bias. Algorithms are not inherently neutral; they are shaped by the data on which they are trained and the objectives they are designed to achieve. If the data used to train an algorithm contains biases or inaccuracies, these can be perpetuated and amplified in the algorithm's outputs. This can result in the unequal representation of certain viewpoints or the prioritization of misleading content, contributing to the spread of misinformation.

Addressing the role of algorithms in spreading misinformation requires a multifaceted approach. One potential solution is to increase transparency in how algorithms operate. By providing users with greater insight into the factors that influence content curation, platforms can empower individuals to make more informed decisions about the information they consume. This could involve offering explanations for why certain content is recommended or providing users with tools to customize their content preferences.

Another strategy is to enhance the accountability of platforms and developers in the design and deployment of algorithms. This could involve establishing industry standards or regulatory frameworks that promote ethical algorithmic practices and prioritize the accuracy and reliability of information. By holding platforms accountable for the impact of their algorithms, it is possible to mitigate the spread of misinformation and promote a more trustworthy information ecosystem.

Education also plays a critical role in addressing the challenges posed by algorithms and misinformation. By fostering digital literacy and critical thinking skills, individuals can become more discerning consumers of information, better equipped to navigate the complexities of the digital landscape. This includes understanding how algorithms influence the content they encounter and developing the ability to critically evaluate the credibility of information sources.

Collaboration between technology companies, policymakers, and civil society is essential in addressing the role of algorithms in spreading misinformation. By working together, stakeholders can develop innovative solutions that balance the benefits of personalized content with the need for accurate and reliable information. This could involve the development of new technologies or initiatives that promote the verification and fact-checking of content, as well as efforts to raise awareness about the impact of algorithms on information dissemination.

The Economics of Fake News Who Profits

Fake news, a term that has become synonymous with misinformation, is not just a social or political issue; it is an economic one as well. The dissemination of false information is often driven by financial incentives, with various actors profiting from its spread. Understanding the economic dynamics behind fake news is crucial to addressing its pervasive influence in our society.

At the core of the fake news economy is the advertising revenue model. Many websites that propagate false information rely on advertising as their primary source of income. These sites generate revenue through pay-per-click or pay-per-impression models, where advertisers pay based on the number of clicks or views their ads receive. The more sensational or controversial the content, the more likely it is to attract clicks, driving traffic to these sites and increasing their advertising revenue. This creates a perverse incentive for content creators to prioritize sensationalism over accuracy, as the financial rewards are directly tied to the volume of traffic generated.

Social media platforms also play a significant role in the economics of fake news. These platforms are designed to maximize user engagement, often through algorithms that prioritize content likely to elicit strong emotional responses. As users engage with sensational or misleading content, it gains visibility and spreads more widely, further increasing its reach and potential for profit. Social media companies benefit financially from this increased engagement, as it translates into higher advertising revenue for the platform. While these companies may not directly profit from fake news, their business models can inadvertently contribute to its proliferation.

The economics of fake news extend beyond advertising revenue. Political actors and interest groups may also exploit misinformation for financial gain. By spreading false narratives, they can influence public opinion, sway elections, or undermine opponents, ultimately achieving political or economic objectives. In some cases, these actors may fund fake news operations directly, providing financial support to websites or individuals who produce and disseminate misleading content. This creates a complex web of financial interests that can be difficult to untangle, as the lines between political and economic motivations are often blurred.

The role of data brokers in the fake news economy is another critical aspect to consider. These entities collect and sell user data to advertisers, political campaigns, and other interested parties. By analyzing user behavior and preferences, data brokers can identify target audiences for specific types of content, including fake news. This information can be used to tailor and distribute misleading content more effectively, increasing its impact and profitability. The sale of user data thus becomes a lucrative business, with data brokers profiting from the spread of misinformation.

Addressing the economics of fake news requires a multifaceted approach. One potential solution is to disrupt the financial incentives that drive the production and dissemination of false information. This could involve implementing stricter regulations on online advertising, such as requiring greater transparency in ad placements or limiting the types of content that can be monetized. By reducing the financial rewards associated with fake news, it may be possible to decrease its prevalence.

Another strategy is to hold social media platforms accountable for the role they play in the spread of misinformation. This could involve implementing policies that promote the accuracy and reliability of content, such as fact-checking initiatives or algorithmic adjustments that prioritize credible sources. By creating an environment where accurate information is more visible and accessible, platforms can help mitigate the impact of fake news on their users.

Education and media literacy are also essential components of addressing the economics of fake news. By equipping individuals with the skills to critically evaluate information and recognize misleading content, it is possible to reduce the demand for fake news and diminish its profitability. This includes fostering an understanding of how financial incentives can influence the information landscape and encouraging users to seek out diverse and credible sources.

Collaboration between governments, technology companies, and civil society is crucial in tackling the economic drivers of fake news. By working together, stakeholders can develop innovative solutions that balance the need for free expression with the imperative to combat misinformation. This could involve the creation of industry standards or regulatory frameworks that promote ethical practices in content creation and distribution, as well as efforts to raise awareness about the financial motivations behind fake news.

Chapter 3

Propaganda Techniques and Tactics

Classic Propaganda Techniques A Primer

Propaganda, a tool as old as civilization itself, has been wielded by leaders, governments, and organizations to shape public perception and influence behavior. Its techniques, honed over centuries, remain relevant in today's media-saturated world. Understanding these classic methods is essential for recognizing and resisting manipulation.

One of the most enduring techniques is the use of emotional appeal. Propagandists tap into the audience's emotions, such as fear, anger, or pride, to elicit a desired response. By crafting messages that resonate on an emotional level, they bypass rational analysis and encourage immediate reactions. This method is particularly effective in times of crisis, where fear can be leveraged to justify drastic measures or rally support for a cause. For instance, wartime propaganda often depicts the enemy as monstrous or subhuman, stoking fear and hatred to galvanize public support for military action.

Another classic technique is the bandwagon effect, which capitalizes on the human tendency to conform to the majority. By presenting an idea or behavior as popular or widely accepted, propagandists create a sense of social pressure to align with the perceived consensus. This method is frequently employed in advertising, where products are marketed as the choice of the masses, encouraging consumers to join the trend. In political contexts, the bandwagon effect can be used to create the illusion of widespread support for a candidate or policy, influencing undecided individuals to follow suit.

The use of testimonials is another powerful propaganda tool. By enlisting respected or influential figures to endorse a message, propagandists lend credibility and authority to their cause. This technique relies on the audience's trust in the endorser, whether it be a celebrity, expert, or community leader. Testimonials can be particularly persuasive when the endorser is perceived as impartial or having firsthand experience with the issue at hand. In the realm of public health, for example, endorsements from medical professionals can be instrumental in promoting vaccination campaigns.

Repetition is a fundamental technique in the propagandist's arsenal. By repeating a message frequently and consistently, propagandists increase its familiarity and perceived truthfulness. This method exploits the psychological phenomenon known as the "illusory truth effect," where repeated statements are more likely to be accepted as true, regardless of their accuracy. Repetition can be seen in political slogans, advertising jingles, and media narratives, where the constant reinforcement of a message shapes public perception over time.

The technique of card stacking involves presenting information selectively to favor a particular viewpoint. By highlighting positive aspects and omitting or downplaying negative ones, propagandists create a biased narrative that supports their agenda. This method can be subtle, involving the careful selection of facts, statistics, or anecdotes that align with the desired message. Card stacking is prevalent in political campaigns, where candidates emphasize their achievements while glossing over controversies or failures.

Name-calling is a technique that seeks to discredit opponents by associating them with negative labels or stereotypes. By attaching derogatory terms to individuals or groups, propagandists aim to evoke prejudice and diminish the credibility of their adversaries. This method relies on the power of language to shape perceptions and can be particularly effective in polarizing environments. Name-calling is often used in political discourse, where opponents are branded with pejorative labels to undermine their legitimacy.

The glittering generalities technique involves the use of vague, positive language to evoke approval without providing substantive information. By employing words with strong emotional connotations, such as "freedom," "justice," or "patriotism," propagandists appeal to shared values and ideals. This method relies on the audience's interpretation of these terms, allowing them to project their own beliefs onto the message. Glittering generalities are common in political speeches and advertising, where they serve to inspire and unify audiences without delving into specifics.

Transfer is a technique that seeks to associate a message with a respected symbol or authority. By linking a cause or product to a revered figure, institution, or concept, propagandists aim to transfer the positive attributes of the symbol to their message. This method can be seen in advertising, where products are associated with national flags, religious symbols, or historical figures to evoke trust and admiration. In political contexts, transfer is used to align candidates or policies with revered leaders or national ideals.

The plain folks technique involves presenting the propagandist or their message as relatable and aligned with the everyday experiences of the audience. By adopting the language, mannerisms, or concerns of ordinary people, propagandists seek to build rapport and trust. This method is often employed by politicians who emphasize their humble origins or connection to the common citizen, positioning themselves as champions of the people's interests. In advertising, plain folks appeals are used to suggest that a product is accessible and suitable for everyone.

Finally, the fear appeal technique leverages the power of fear to motivate action or compliance. By presenting a threat or danger, propagandists create a sense of urgency and compel the audience to respond. This method is effective in situations where the perceived risk is high, and the proposed solution is framed as the only viable option. Fear appeals are commonly used in public health campaigns, where the consequences of inaction are emphasized to encourage preventive measures.

Modern Propaganda in the Digital Age

In the digital age, propaganda has evolved into a sophisticated and pervasive force, seamlessly integrated into the fabric of our online lives. The internet, with its vast reach and immediacy, has transformed the way information is disseminated and consumed, creating fertile ground for modern propaganda techniques. Understanding these methods is crucial for navigating the complex landscape of digital media and safeguarding oneself against manipulation.

One of the most significant developments in modern propaganda is the use of social media platforms as vehicles for influence. These platforms, with their billions of users, provide propagandists with unprecedented access to diverse audiences. By leveraging algorithms that prioritize engagement, propagandists can amplify their messages, ensuring they reach a wide and receptive audience. The viral nature of social media allows for rapid dissemination of information, making it an ideal tool for spreading propaganda. This is particularly evident in the use of memes and viral content, which distill complex ideas into easily digestible and shareable formats, often laden with emotional or ideological undertones.

The rise of fake news and misinformation is another hallmark of digital-age propaganda. With the democratization of content creation, anyone with an internet connection can produce and distribute information, blurring the lines between credible journalism and fabricated stories. Propagandists exploit this ambiguity by creating and disseminating false or misleading information to shape public perception. These efforts are often coordinated, involving networks of websites, social media accounts, and bots that work in concert to amplify false narratives. The sheer volume of information online makes it challenging for individuals to discern truth from fiction, allowing propaganda to thrive in the digital ecosystem.

Microtargeting is a technique that has gained prominence in the digital age, enabled by the vast amounts of data collected by online platforms. By analyzing users' online behavior, preferences, and demographics, propagandists can tailor messages to specific audiences, increasing their effectiveness. This personalized approach allows for the delivery of highly relevant content that resonates with individuals on a personal level, bypassing traditional gatekeepers of information. Microtargeting is particularly prevalent in political campaigns, where candidates use data-driven strategies to reach potential voters with customized messages designed to sway their opinions or mobilize them to action.

The use of bots and automated accounts is another modern propaganda tactic that has gained traction in the digital age. These automated entities can generate and spread content at an unprecedented scale, creating the illusion of widespread support or consensus. By flooding social media platforms with coordinated messages, bots can manipulate public discourse, drown out dissenting voices, and create echo chambers that reinforce specific narratives. This technique is often employed in political contexts, where bots are used to amplify partisan messages, attack opponents, or sow discord among the electorate.

Astroturfing, a practice that involves creating the appearance of grassroots support for a cause or movement, has also been adapted for the digital age. Propagandists use fake accounts, paid influencers, and coordinated campaigns to simulate organic public engagement, lending credibility and legitimacy to their messages. This manufactured support can sway public opinion, influence policy decisions, and create a bandwagon effect, where individuals are more likely to support a cause they perceive as popular. Astroturfing is particularly effective in online environments, where the anonymity and reach of the internet make it difficult to distinguish genuine grassroots movements from orchestrated campaigns.

The digital age has also seen the emergence of deepfakes and manipulated media as tools of propaganda. These technologies allow for the creation of realistic but fabricated audio and video content, blurring the line between reality and fiction. Deepfakes can be used to impersonate public figures, spread false information, or create damaging narratives, posing significant challenges to media literacy and trust. The potential for deepfakes to deceive and manipulate is vast, making them a potent weapon in the arsenal of modern propagandists.

Countering modern propaganda in the digital age requires a multifaceted approach that combines media literacy, critical thinking, and technological solutions. Individuals must develop the skills to critically evaluate the information they encounter, questioning the sources, motives, and credibility of the content they consume. This involves recognizing the signs of propaganda, such as emotional appeals, biased narratives, and the use of manipulative techniques.

Technological solutions, such as fact-checking tools, content moderation algorithms, and digital literacy programs, play a crucial role in combating digital-age propaganda. These tools can help identify and flag false or misleading information, providing users with the resources to make informed decisions. Collaboration between technology companies, governments, and civil society is essential to develop and implement effective strategies for addressing the challenges posed by modern propaganda.

The Use of Emotional Appeals in Propaganda

Emotional appeals have long been a cornerstone of propaganda, wielded with precision to sway public opinion and influence behavior. In the digital age, where information is abundant and attention spans are fleeting, the potency of emotional appeals has only intensified. By tapping into the core of human emotions, propagandists can bypass rational thought, creating visceral reactions that drive individuals to action or inaction. Understanding the mechanisms and effects of emotional appeals is crucial for recognizing and resisting their influence.

At the heart of emotional appeals lies the ability to evoke strong feelings, whether it be fear, anger, hope, or pride. These emotions are powerful motivators, capable of overriding logic and reason. Fear, for instance, is a primal emotion that can trigger immediate responses. Propagandists often exploit fear by presenting threats, real or imagined, to provoke anxiety and urgency. This tactic is evident in political campaigns that emphasize national security threats or economic instability, compelling individuals to support policies or candidates that promise safety and stability.

Anger is another emotion frequently harnessed in propaganda. By identifying and vilifying an enemy or scapegoat, propagandists can channel public frustration and resentment towards a common target. This technique fosters a sense of unity and purpose among supporters, while simultaneously dehumanizing and marginalizing the opposition. Historical examples abound, from wartime propaganda that demonizes the enemy to modern political rhetoric that pits one group against another. The resulting polarization can deepen societal divides, making it challenging to find common ground or engage in constructive dialogue.

Hope and optimism, on the other hand, are emotions that can inspire and uplift. Propagandists use these appeals to paint a vision of a better future, promising progress, prosperity, or justice. By tapping into individuals' aspirations and desires, these messages can galvanize support for movements, ideologies, or leaders. The civil rights movement, for example, effectively used hopeful narratives to rally support for social change, emphasizing the possibility of a more equitable and inclusive society. In the digital age, these appeals are often disseminated through inspirational stories, viral campaigns, and charismatic leaders who embody the promise of a brighter tomorrow.

Pride and identity are also central to emotional appeals in propaganda. By appealing to individuals' sense of belonging and self-worth, propagandists can foster loyalty and allegiance. Nationalistic propaganda, for instance, often emphasizes cultural heritage, historical achievements, and national pride to rally citizens around a common identity. This sense of pride can be a powerful motivator, encouraging individuals to support policies or actions that align with their perceived identity. In the digital realm, identity-based appeals are amplified through social media, where communities form around shared values, beliefs, or interests.

The effectiveness of emotional appeals in propaganda is further enhanced by the use of storytelling techniques. Stories have a unique ability to engage emotions, making abstract concepts relatable and memorable. By weaving narratives that resonate with individuals' experiences or values, propagandists can create a sense of connection and empathy. These stories often feature relatable characters, compelling conflicts, and satisfying resolutions, drawing audiences into a narrative that reinforces the desired message. In the digital age, storytelling is a powerful tool for creating viral content, as stories are easily shared and consumed across platforms.

Visual imagery is another potent element of emotional appeals. Images have an immediate impact, capable of conveying complex emotions and messages in an instant. Propagandists use visuals to evoke strong emotional responses, whether it be through powerful photographs, evocative symbols, or striking graphics. The iconic image of a lone protester standing before a tank, for example, captures the essence of courage and defiance, resonating with audiences worldwide. In the digital age, visual content is ubiquitous, with platforms like Instagram and TikTok prioritizing images and videos that capture attention and elicit emotional reactions.

To counter the influence of emotional appeals in propaganda, individuals must cultivate media literacy and critical thinking skills. This involves recognizing the emotional triggers embedded in messages and questioning the motives behind them. By understanding the techniques used to manipulate emotions, individuals can make more informed decisions and resist the pull of propaganda. It is also essential to seek diverse perspectives and engage in open dialogue, challenging the narratives that seek to divide or manipulate.

Education plays a vital role in building resilience against emotional appeals. By teaching individuals to analyze and evaluate media content, educators can empower them to navigate the complex landscape of digital information. This includes understanding the role of emotions in communication, recognizing bias and manipulation, and developing the ability to articulate and defend one's beliefs. Collaborative efforts between educators, media organizations, and policymakers are necessary to create a media-literate society capable of resisting the influence of propaganda.

Analyzing Political Propaganda Campaigns

Political propaganda campaigns have been a fixture in shaping public opinion and influencing electoral outcomes throughout history. These campaigns employ a variety of strategies and techniques to persuade, manipulate, and mobilize the masses. Understanding the anatomy of political propaganda is essential for discerning the underlying motives and messages that drive these campaigns. By dissecting the components and tactics used, individuals can better navigate the complex landscape of political communication.

At the core of any political propaganda campaign is the message. This message is crafted to resonate with the target audience, often appealing to their values, beliefs, and emotions. The message is typically simple, memorable, and repeated frequently to ensure it sticks in the minds of the public. Slogans, soundbites, and catchphrases are common tools used to distill complex ideas into digestible and impactful statements. These messages are designed to evoke emotional responses, whether it be hope, fear, anger, or pride, and are often tailored to align with the prevailing sentiments of the time.

The messenger is equally important in political propaganda campaigns. Charismatic leaders, trusted figures, and influential personalities are often enlisted to deliver the message, lending credibility and authority to the campaign. The choice of messenger can significantly impact the effectiveness of the propaganda, as individuals are more likely to be persuaded by someone they admire or trust. In some cases, the messenger may be a symbolic figurehead, representing the ideals and aspirations of the campaign, while in others, they may be a relatable and approachable spokesperson who connects with the audience on a personal level.

Media plays a pivotal role in the dissemination of political propaganda. Traditional media outlets, such as newspapers, television, and radio, have long been used to broadcast campaign messages to a wide audience. However, the rise of digital media has transformed the landscape of political communication, enabling campaigns to reach individuals directly through social media platforms, websites, and online advertisements. This shift has allowed for more targeted and personalized messaging, as campaigns can tailor their content to specific demographics, interests, and behaviors. The use of data analytics and algorithms has further enhanced the precision and effectiveness of digital propaganda, enabling campaigns to optimize their strategies in real-time.

Visual imagery is another powerful tool in political propaganda campaigns. Images, videos, and graphics can convey complex messages and emotions in an instant, making them an effective means of capturing attention and eliciting responses. Campaigns often use visual elements to reinforce their messages, create associations, and evoke emotional reactions. Iconic images, such as campaign posters, logos, and symbols, can become synonymous with the campaign itself, serving as a visual shorthand for its ideals and objectives. In the digital age, visual content is easily shared and disseminated, amplifying its reach and impact.

Narratives and storytelling are central to the success of political propaganda campaigns. By crafting compelling stories that resonate with the audience, campaigns can create a sense of connection and empathy. These narratives often feature relatable characters, conflicts, and resolutions, drawing individuals into a storyline that reinforces the campaign's message. The use of anecdotes, testimonials, and personal stories can humanize the campaign, making it more relatable and engaging. In some cases, campaigns may employ fictional or exaggerated narratives to dramatize their message and capture the public's imagination.

The timing and context of a political propaganda campaign are crucial factors in its effectiveness. Campaigns are often strategically timed to coincide with key events, such as elections, debates, or crises, to maximize their impact. The context in which the campaign is launched can also influence its reception, as prevailing social, economic, and political conditions can shape public perceptions and attitudes. By aligning their message with the current zeitgeist, campaigns can tap into existing sentiments and concerns, making their propaganda more relevant and persuasive.

To critically analyze political propaganda campaigns, individuals must develop media literacy and critical thinking skills. This involves questioning the motives behind the message, evaluating the credibility of the messenger, and scrutinizing the techniques used to persuade and manipulate. By understanding the strategies and tactics employed in propaganda, individuals can make more informed decisions and resist the influence of manipulative campaigns. It is also important to seek diverse perspectives and engage in open dialogue, challenging the narratives that seek to divide or polarize.

Education is a key component in building resilience against political propaganda. By teaching individuals to analyze and evaluate media content, educators can empower them to navigate the complex landscape of political communication. This includes understanding the role of emotions in persuasion, recognizing bias and manipulation, and developing the ability to articulate and defend one's beliefs. Collaborative efforts between educators, media organizations, and policymakers are necessary to create a media-literate society capable of resisting the influence of propaganda.

Propaganda in Advertising and Marketing

Propaganda in advertising and marketing is a pervasive force that shapes consumer behavior and influences purchasing decisions. By employing persuasive techniques and strategic messaging, advertisers and marketers craft campaigns that resonate with target audiences, often blurring the line between information and manipulation. Understanding the mechanisms of propaganda in this context is crucial for consumers to make informed choices and for businesses to engage ethically with their audiences.

At the heart of advertising and marketing propaganda lies the art of persuasion. Advertisers use a variety of techniques to capture attention, evoke emotions, and create desire for products or services. One common method is the use of emotional appeals, which tap into feelings such as happiness, fear, nostalgia, or aspiration. By associating a product with positive emotions or experiences, advertisers create a powerful connection that can drive consumer behavior. For example, a commercial for a luxury car might emphasize the thrill of driving and the status it confers, appealing to consumers' desires for excitement and prestige.

Another key element of propaganda in advertising is the creation of a compelling narrative. Storytelling is a powerful tool that allows brands to communicate their values, mission, and identity in a relatable and engaging way. By crafting stories that resonate with consumers' experiences and aspirations, advertisers can build brand loyalty and foster a sense of community. These narratives often feature relatable characters, conflicts, and resolutions, drawing consumers into a storyline that reinforces the brand's message. For instance, a campaign for a fitness brand might tell the story of an individual's journey to health and wellness, inspiring consumers to embark on their own fitness journeys.

The use of repetition is another hallmark of advertising propaganda. By consistently repeating key messages, slogans, or images, advertisers ensure that their brand remains top-of-mind for consumers. This repetition creates familiarity and reinforces brand recognition, making it more likely that consumers will choose the advertised product when making purchasing decisions. The iconic "Just Do It" slogan by Nike is a prime example of how repetition can cement a brand's message in the public consciousness.

Social proof is a powerful psychological phenomenon that advertisers leverage to influence consumer behavior. By showcasing testimonials, reviews, or endorsements from satisfied customers or influential figures, advertisers create the perception that a product is popular and trustworthy. This technique taps into consumers' natural tendency to conform to social norms and seek validation from others. For example, a skincare brand might feature testimonials from dermatologists or celebrities, lending credibility and authority to their claims.

Scarcity is another tactic used in advertising propaganda to create urgency and drive sales. By suggesting that a product is in limited supply or available for a limited time, advertisers create a sense of urgency that compels consumers to act quickly. This technique plays on the fear of missing out, prompting consumers to make impulsive purchasing decisions. Limited-time offers, flash sales, and exclusive releases are common examples of how scarcity is used to influence consumer behavior.

Visual imagery is a powerful component of advertising propaganda, as it can convey complex messages and emotions in an instant. Advertisers use images, colors, and design elements to create associations and evoke emotional responses. For example, the use of vibrant colors and dynamic imagery in a sports drink advertisement can convey energy and vitality, appealing to consumers' desires for an active lifestyle. Visual elements are also used to create brand identity and recognition, with logos and packaging playing a crucial role in differentiating products in a crowded marketplace.

The rise of digital media has transformed the landscape of advertising and marketing, enabling brands to reach consumers directly through social media platforms, websites, and online advertisements. This shift has allowed for more targeted and personalized messaging, as advertisers can tailor their content to specific demographics, interests, and behaviors. The use of data analytics and algorithms has further enhanced the precision and effectiveness of digital advertising, enabling brands to optimize their strategies in real-time. However, this also raises ethical concerns about privacy and data usage, as consumers may be unaware of the extent to which their information is being used to influence their behavior.

To critically analyze advertising and marketing propaganda, consumers must develop media literacy and critical thinking skills. This involves questioning the motives behind the message, evaluating the credibility of the source, and scrutinizing the techniques used to persuade and manipulate. By understanding the strategies and tactics employed in advertising, consumers can make more informed decisions and resist the influence of manipulative campaigns. It is also important to seek diverse perspectives and engage in open dialogue, challenging the narratives that seek to shape consumer behavior.

For businesses, ethical advertising practices are essential for building trust and maintaining a positive brand reputation. This includes being transparent about the intentions and claims of advertising campaigns, respecting consumer privacy, and avoiding deceptive or misleading tactics. By prioritizing authenticity and integrity, businesses can foster long-term relationships with their customers and contribute to a more ethical and responsible advertising landscape.

Chapter 4

The Role of Social Media in Media Manipulation

Social Media Platforms as Information Gatekeepers

Social media platforms have emerged as powerful information gatekeepers in the digital age, shaping the way we access, consume, and share information. These platforms, with their vast user bases and sophisticated algorithms, have transformed the landscape of communication, influencing public discourse and societal norms. As information gatekeepers, social media platforms wield significant power in determining what content is visible, how it is prioritized, and who has access to it.

The role of social media platforms as information gatekeepers is largely driven by algorithms that curate content for users. These algorithms analyze user behavior, preferences, and interactions to deliver personalized content feeds. While this personalization enhances user experience by presenting relevant content, it also creates echo chambers where users are exposed to information that reinforces their existing beliefs. This phenomenon can lead to polarization, as individuals are less likely to encounter diverse perspectives or engage with opposing viewpoints.

The power of social media platforms as gatekeepers is further amplified by their ability to amplify certain voices and suppress others. Through features such as trending topics, hashtags, and promoted content, platforms can elevate specific narratives and shape public discourse. This amplification can be beneficial in raising awareness for important issues or movements, but it also raises concerns about the potential for manipulation and bias. For instance, the use of bots or coordinated campaigns to artificially inflate the visibility of certain content can distort public perception and influence opinions.

Content moderation is another critical aspect of social media platforms' role as information gatekeepers. Platforms are tasked with enforcing community guidelines and removing harmful or inappropriate content. However, the scale and complexity of this task present significant challenges. The sheer volume of content generated daily makes it difficult to monitor and moderate effectively, leading to inconsistencies and errors. Additionally, the subjective nature of content moderation decisions can result in accusations of censorship or bias, as users may perceive certain actions as unfair or politically motivated.

The spread of misinformation and disinformation on social media platforms underscores the importance of their role as information gatekeepers. False or misleading information can spread rapidly, fueled by the viral nature of social media and the tendency for sensational content to attract attention. This poses significant risks to public health, safety, and democracy, as misinformation can influence behavior, erode trust in institutions, and undermine informed decision-making. Platforms have implemented various measures to combat misinformation, such as fact-checking partnerships, warning labels, and content removal. However, the effectiveness of these measures is often debated, and the balance between free expression and responsible information dissemination remains a contentious issue.

The influence of social media platforms as information gatekeepers extends beyond individual users to impact media organizations and journalism. Traditional media outlets increasingly rely on social media for distribution and audience engagement, adapting their content to fit platform algorithms and user preferences. This shift has implications for journalistic integrity and editorial independence, as the pressure to generate clicks and shares can lead to sensationalism or the prioritization of entertainment over substantive reporting. Moreover, the decline of traditional revenue models has led to increased reliance on social media platforms for advertising, further entrenching their role as gatekeepers in the media ecosystem.

The global reach of social media platforms presents unique challenges and opportunities in their role as information gatekeepers. Cultural, linguistic, and regulatory differences across regions necessitate tailored approaches to content moderation and policy enforcement. Platforms must navigate complex legal and ethical landscapes, balancing local norms and laws with universal principles of free expression and human rights. This requires collaboration with governments, civil society, and other stakeholders to develop frameworks that promote transparency, accountability, and inclusivity.

As users, we play a crucial role in shaping the influence of social media platforms as information gatekeepers. By critically evaluating the content we consume and share, we can mitigate the impact of misinformation and contribute to a more informed and diverse online environment. This involves questioning the sources and credibility of information, seeking out diverse perspectives, and engaging in constructive dialogue. Media literacy and digital citizenship education are essential tools in empowering individuals to navigate the complexities of the digital information landscape.

For social media platforms, transparency and accountability are key to fulfilling their responsibilities as information gatekeepers. This includes providing clear and accessible information about content moderation policies, algorithmic processes, and data usage. Platforms should engage with users, experts, and stakeholders to develop and refine policies that reflect diverse perspectives and address emerging challenges. By fostering an open and collaborative approach, platforms can build trust and credibility with their users and contribute to a healthier information ecosystem.

Viral Misinformation How It Spreads

In the digital age, the rapid spread of information across the globe is both a marvel and a menace. Viral misinformation, in particular, poses a significant challenge, as it can disseminate falsehoods at an alarming pace, often outstripping the reach of factual information. Understanding how misinformation spreads is crucial to combating its effects and fostering a more informed society.

The anatomy of viral misinformation is complex, involving a confluence of psychological, technological, and social factors. At its core, misinformation thrives on the human propensity for cognitive biases. Confirmation bias, for instance, leads individuals to favor information that aligns with their pre-existing beliefs, while the availability heuristic makes people more likely to believe information that is easily retrievable from memory. These biases create fertile ground for misinformation to take root and flourish.

Social media platforms serve as the primary conduits for the spread of misinformation, leveraging their vast networks and sophisticated algorithms. These platforms are designed to maximize user engagement, often prioritizing sensational or emotionally charged content that captures attention. Misinformation, with its often provocative or shocking nature, fits this mold perfectly, making it more likely to be shared and amplified. The viral nature of social media means that misinformation can reach millions of users within hours, creating a ripple effect that is difficult to contain.

The role of influencers and opinion leaders in the spread of misinformation cannot be overstated. Individuals with large followings or perceived authority can significantly impact the dissemination of information, whether intentionally or inadvertently. When influencers share misinformation, it gains credibility and visibility, encouraging their followers to further propagate it.

This phenomenon is exacerbated by the echo chamber effect, where users are primarily exposed to information that reinforces their existing views, limiting their exposure to corrective or diverse perspectives.

The emotional appeal of misinformation is another factor contributing to its virality. Content that evokes strong emotions, such as fear, anger, or empathy, is more likely to be shared, as people are driven to react and engage with emotionally charged material. Misinformation often exploits these emotions, using sensational headlines or narratives to capture attention and provoke a response. This emotional engagement can override critical thinking, leading individuals to share content without verifying its accuracy.

The anonymity and speed of online communication also play a role in the spread of misinformation. The lack of face-to-face interaction reduces accountability, allowing individuals to share false information with little fear of repercussions. Additionally, the rapid pace of information exchange on digital platforms encourages impulsive sharing, as users may prioritize immediacy over accuracy. This environment creates a perfect storm for misinformation to proliferate unchecked.

Efforts to combat the spread of misinformation must address these underlying factors. Media literacy education is a critical tool in empowering individuals to critically evaluate the information they encounter. By teaching people to recognize cognitive biases, assess the credibility of sources, and verify facts, media literacy can reduce the susceptibility to misinformation. Encouraging skepticism and critical thinking can help individuals resist the allure of sensational content and make more informed decisions about what to share.

Social media platforms also have a responsibility to mitigate the spread of misinformation. Implementing robust content moderation policies, promoting credible sources, and providing users with tools to report false information are essential steps in curbing misinformation. Transparency in algorithmic processes and collaboration with fact-checking organizations can enhance the effectiveness of these measures. Platforms must balance the need for open expression with the imperative to prevent harm caused by misinformation.

The role of governments and regulatory bodies in addressing misinformation is a subject of ongoing debate. While some advocate for stricter regulations and penalties for spreading false information, others caution against potential infringements on free speech. A balanced approach that respects individual rights while promoting accountability and transparency is necessary. Governments can support media literacy initiatives, fund research on misinformation, and facilitate collaboration between stakeholders to develop comprehensive strategies.

Individuals, too, have a role to play in combating misinformation. By cultivating a habit of critical inquiry and skepticism, people can become more discerning consumers of information. Taking the time to verify facts, cross-check sources, and consider alternative viewpoints can reduce the likelihood of sharing misinformation. Engaging in constructive dialogue and challenging false narratives within one's social circles can also contribute to a more informed community.

The Influence of Social Media Influencers

In the digital landscape, social media influencers have emerged as powerful figures, shaping opinions, trends, and consumer behavior. Their influence extends across various platforms, reaching millions of followers who look to them for guidance, inspiration, and entertainment. Understanding the dynamics of influencer impact is crucial for anyone navigating the modern world, whether as a consumer, marketer, or content creator.

At the heart of an influencer's power lies their ability to connect with audiences on a personal level. Unlike traditional celebrities, influencers often cultivate a sense of intimacy and relatability with their followers. They share glimpses of their daily lives, personal struggles, and triumphs, creating a bond that feels authentic and genuine. This connection fosters trust, making followers more receptive to the influencer's recommendations and opinions.

The rise of influencers can be attributed to the democratization of content creation. Social media platforms have lowered the barriers to entry, allowing individuals from diverse backgrounds to share their voices and build audiences. This accessibility has led to a proliferation of niche influencers, each catering to specific interests and communities. From beauty and fashion to fitness and gaming, influencers cover a vast array of topics, providing tailored content that resonates with their followers.

The impact of influencers is particularly pronounced in the realm of consumer behavior. Brands recognize the persuasive power of influencers and often collaborate with them to promote products and services. Influencer marketing has become a multi-billion-dollar industry, with companies leveraging the reach and credibility of influencers to drive sales and brand awareness. The authenticity of influencer endorsements can be more compelling than traditional advertising, as followers perceive them as genuine recommendations rather than paid promotions.

However, the relationship between influencers and their audiences is not without challenges. The line between authenticity and commercialization can blur, leading to skepticism among followers. As influencers engage in more brand partnerships, they risk alienating their audience if they are perceived as prioritizing profit over genuine connection. Transparency and honesty are crucial in maintaining trust, and influencers must navigate the delicate balance between monetization and authenticity.

The influence of social media personalities extends beyond consumer behavior, impacting societal norms and cultural trends. Influencers have the power to shape public discourse, raise awareness about social issues, and drive movements. Their platforms provide a space for marginalized voices to be heard, amplifying causes that may otherwise go unnoticed. Influencers can inspire change by using their reach to advocate for social justice, environmental sustainability, and other important issues.

Yet, with great power comes great responsibility. The content shared by influencers can have far-reaching consequences, influencing the beliefs and behaviors of their followers. Misinformation, harmful stereotypes, and unrealistic standards can proliferate if influencers are not mindful of their impact. It is essential for influencers to approach their platforms with a sense of responsibility, recognizing the potential influence they wield over their audience.

For aspiring influencers, building a successful presence requires more than just a large following. Authenticity, consistency, and engagement are key components of a thriving influencer career. Aspiring influencers should focus on creating content that reflects their genuine interests and values, fostering a community that shares their passions. Engaging with followers through comments, direct messages, and live interactions can strengthen the bond between influencer and audience, enhancing loyalty and trust.

The role of social media platforms in shaping influencer culture cannot be overlooked. Algorithms, monetization policies, and platform features all play a role in determining which influencers rise to prominence. Platforms have a responsibility to create an environment that supports diverse voices and promotes ethical content creation. By prioritizing transparency and accountability, platforms can contribute to a healthier influencer ecosystem.

For brands and marketers, collaborating with influencers requires careful consideration and strategy. Selecting the right influencer involves assessing their audience demographics, engagement rates, and alignment with brand values. Authentic partnerships that resonate with both the influencer's audience and the brand's target market are more likely to succeed. Clear communication and mutual respect are essential in fostering productive collaborations that benefit both parties.

The Role of Bots and Trolls in Manipulating Discourse

In the vast expanse of the digital world, where conversations unfold at lightning speed and information flows ceaselessly, the presence of bots and trolls has become an undeniable force. These digital entities, often shrouded in anonymity, wield significant power in shaping and manipulating discourse across social media platforms, forums, and comment sections. Understanding their role is crucial for anyone seeking to navigate the complexities of online communication and discern truth from manipulation.

Bots, short for robots, are automated programs designed to perform specific tasks on the internet. They can be programmed to post content, engage with users, and even simulate human-like interactions. While some bots serve benign purposes, such as providing customer support or disseminating news updates, others are deployed with more insidious intentions. Malicious bots can flood platforms with spam, spread misinformation, and amplify divisive content, all while operating at a scale and speed that far surpasses human capabilities.

The impact of bots on online discourse is multifaceted. One of their primary functions is to create the illusion of consensus or popularity. By generating a high volume of likes, shares, or comments, bots can artificially inflate the perceived support for a particular viewpoint or agenda. This manufactured consensus can sway public opinion, influence trending topics, and even affect the outcomes of elections or policy decisions. The sheer volume of bot activity can drown out genuine voices, making it challenging for users to discern authentic discourse from orchestrated manipulation.

Trolls, on the other hand, are human users who deliberately provoke, harass, or disrupt online conversations. Unlike bots, trolls thrive on eliciting emotional reactions from their targets, often employing inflammatory language, personal attacks, or divisive rhetoric. Their motivations can vary, ranging from amusement and attention-seeking to advancing political or ideological agendas. Trolls can derail meaningful discussions, create hostile environments, and contribute to the polarization of online communities.

The tactics employed by trolls are diverse and adaptable. They may impersonate others, spread false information, or engage in coordinated campaigns to target specific individuals or groups. Trolls often exploit the anonymity afforded by the internet, allowing them to operate without fear of accountability. This anonymity can embolden individuals to engage in behavior they might otherwise avoid in face-to-face interactions, leading to a proliferation of toxic discourse.

The interplay between bots and trolls can amplify their collective impact on online discourse. Bots can be used to support troll campaigns, generating fake engagement or disseminating troll-generated content to a wider audience. This synergy can create a feedback loop, where the actions of bots and trolls reinforce each other, further distorting the digital landscape.

The consequences of bot and troll activity extend beyond individual platforms, affecting broader societal dynamics. The spread of misinformation and divisive content can erode trust in institutions, media, and even interpersonal relationships. As users become more skeptical of the information they encounter online, the potential for constructive dialogue diminishes, giving way to cynicism and disengagement.

For individuals seeking to navigate this complex environment, critical thinking and digital literacy are essential tools. Recognizing the signs of bot and troll activity can help users identify and counteract manipulation. Bots often exhibit patterns of behavior that differ from genuine users, such as posting at regular intervals, lacking personal details, or engaging in repetitive interactions. Trolls, meanwhile, may use inflammatory language, target specific individuals, or consistently disrupt conversations.

Engaging with content critically involves questioning the source, verifying information through multiple channels, and considering the motivations behind the messages encountered online. By fostering a culture of skepticism and inquiry, users can resist the influence of bots and trolls, contributing to a more informed and resilient digital community.

Platforms also play a crucial role in addressing the challenges posed by bots and trolls. Implementing robust moderation policies, employing advanced detection algorithms, and promoting transparency can help mitigate the impact of malicious activity. Collaboration between platforms, researchers, and policymakers is essential in developing comprehensive strategies to combat the manipulation of online discourse.

Efforts to Combat Misinformation on Social Media

In the digital age, social media platforms have become the primary arenas for the exchange of information, ideas, and opinions. However, the rapid dissemination of content has also given rise to a significant challenge: the spread of misinformation. This phenomenon, characterized by the distribution of false or misleading information, poses a threat to public discourse, democracy, and societal trust. As misinformation continues to proliferate, various stakeholders, including social media companies, governments, and civil society organizations, have undertaken efforts to combat its spread and mitigate its impact.

Social media companies, as the custodians of digital platforms, bear a significant responsibility in addressing misinformation. Many have implemented measures to identify and limit the reach of false content. One common approach is the use of algorithms and machine learning models to detect and flag potentially misleading information. These systems analyze patterns, keywords, and user interactions to identify content that may require further scrutiny. Once flagged, content can be subjected to fact-checking by independent organizations, which assess its accuracy and provide context or corrections as needed.

Fact-checking initiatives have become a cornerstone of efforts to combat misinformation. Collaborations between social media platforms and fact-checking organizations have led to the development of comprehensive databases that track and verify claims circulating online. When a piece of content is deemed false or misleading, platforms may apply warning labels, reduce its visibility, or provide users with links to verified information. These measures aim to inform users and encourage critical engagement with the content they encounter.

In addition to technological solutions, social media companies have invested in user education and digital literacy programs. By equipping users with the skills to critically evaluate information, these initiatives empower individuals to discern credible sources from unreliable ones. Educational campaigns often emphasize the importance of cross-referencing information, recognizing biases, and understanding the motivations behind certain narratives. By fostering a more informed user base, platforms hope to reduce the susceptibility of individuals to misinformation.

Governments around the world have also taken steps to address the spread of misinformation on social media. Legislative measures, such as the introduction of laws and regulations, aim to hold platforms accountable for the content shared on their sites. Some governments have mandated transparency in advertising, requiring platforms to disclose the sources and funding behind political ads. Others have imposed penalties for the deliberate dissemination of false information, targeting individuals or entities that engage in coordinated misinformation campaigns.

However, the role of government in combating misinformation is not without controversy. Critics argue that excessive regulation may infringe on freedom of speech and lead to censorship. Striking a balance between curbing misinformation and preserving democratic values remains a complex challenge. To navigate this delicate terrain, some governments have opted for collaborative approaches, working alongside social media companies, researchers, and civil society organizations to develop comprehensive strategies that respect individual rights while addressing the issue at hand.

Civil society organizations, including non-profits, advocacy groups, and academic institutions, play a crucial role in the fight against misinformation. These entities often conduct research to understand the dynamics of misinformation, its sources, and its impact on society. By analyzing trends and patterns, they provide valuable insights that inform policy decisions and platform interventions. Additionally, civil society organizations engage in public awareness campaigns, highlighting the importance of media literacy and encouraging responsible information consumption.

One notable example of civil society involvement is the creation of community-driven fact-checking initiatives. These grassroots efforts leverage the collective knowledge and expertise of volunteers to verify claims and debunk falsehoods. By harnessing the power of crowdsourcing, these initiatives can quickly respond to emerging misinformation and provide timely corrections. The collaborative nature of these projects fosters a sense of shared responsibility and empowers individuals to take an active role in combating misinformation.

Despite the concerted efforts of various stakeholders, the battle against misinformation is far from over. The ever-evolving nature of digital communication presents ongoing challenges, as new platforms, technologies, and tactics emerge. Misinformation can adapt and spread rapidly, often outpacing the mechanisms designed to counter it. As such, continuous innovation and adaptation are essential to staying ahead of the curve.

Looking to the future, the fight against misinformation will likely require a multifaceted approach that combines technological solutions, regulatory frameworks, and public engagement. Collaboration between stakeholders will be key to developing effective strategies that address the root causes of misinformation while respecting fundamental rights and freedoms. By fostering a culture of transparency, accountability, and critical

thinking, society can work towards a more informed
and resilient digital landscape.

Chapter 5

The Impact of Media Manipulation on Democracy

Media Manipulation and Electoral Processes

The integrity of electoral processes is a cornerstone of democratic societies, yet it faces significant challenges in the digital age. Media manipulation has emerged as a potent tool capable of influencing public perception and, ultimately, the outcomes of elections. This manipulation takes various forms, from the dissemination of false information to the strategic framing of narratives, all designed to sway voters and undermine the democratic process. Understanding the mechanisms of media manipulation and its impact on elections is crucial for safeguarding democracy.

One of the most prevalent forms of media manipulation in electoral contexts is the spread of disinformation. This involves the deliberate creation and distribution of false or misleading information with the intent to deceive. Disinformation campaigns often target specific demographics, exploiting existing biases and fears to amplify their impact. These campaigns can be orchestrated by political actors, foreign entities, or interest groups seeking to influence the electoral outcome in their favor.

The digital landscape provides fertile ground for disinformation to flourish. Social media platforms, with their vast reach and rapid dissemination capabilities, serve as ideal conduits for spreading false narratives. The viral nature of social media allows disinformation to reach millions of users within a short span, often outpacing efforts to debunk or counteract it. Moreover, the algorithms that govern content visibility on these platforms can inadvertently amplify sensational or polarizing content, further exacerbating the spread of disinformation.

In addition to disinformation, media manipulation during elections can involve the strategic framing of narratives. This technique involves presenting information in a way that emphasizes certain aspects while downplaying or omitting others. By controlling the narrative, manipulators can shape public perception and influence voter behavior. For instance, a political campaign might focus on highlighting the perceived failures of an opponent while minimizing their own shortcomings, thereby swaying public opinion in their favor.

The use of deepfakes and other forms of synthetic media represents another dimension of media manipulation in electoral processes. Deepfakes are digitally altered videos or audio recordings that convincingly depict individuals saying or doing things they never actually did. These manipulated media can be used to discredit political opponents, spread false information, or create confusion among voters. The realistic nature of deepfakes makes them particularly insidious, as they can be difficult to detect and debunk.

Media manipulation is not limited to digital platforms; traditional media outlets can also play a role in shaping electoral outcomes. Bias in reporting, whether intentional or unintentional, can influence public perception and voter behavior. The selection of stories, the framing of headlines, and the choice of language all contribute to the narrative presented to the public. In some cases, media outlets may align with specific political agendas, further complicating the landscape of information available to voters.

The impact of media manipulation on electoral processes is profound. It can erode public trust in democratic institutions, create divisions within society, and ultimately undermine the legitimacy of election outcomes. When voters are exposed to manipulated information, their ability to make informed decisions is compromised. This can lead to skewed electoral results that do not accurately reflect the will of the people.

Efforts to combat media manipulation in electoral contexts are multifaceted and involve various stakeholders. Governments, media organizations, and civil society groups all play a role in addressing this challenge. Legislative measures, such as transparency requirements for political advertising and penalties for spreading false information, aim to hold actors accountable and deter manipulation. Media literacy programs seek to equip citizens with the skills to critically evaluate information and recognize manipulation tactics.

Social media platforms have also taken steps to address media manipulation during elections. Many have implemented policies to identify and remove false information, particularly when it pertains to electoral processes. Fact-checking partnerships and the use of warning labels are common strategies employed to inform users and reduce the spread of disinformation. However, the effectiveness of these measures is often debated, as manipulators continue to adapt and find new ways to circumvent detection.

International cooperation is essential in addressing media manipulation in electoral processes. Given the global nature of digital communication, disinformation campaigns can originate from foreign actors seeking to influence elections in other countries. Collaborative efforts between nations, such as information sharing and joint investigations, can help identify and counteract these threats. Additionally, international organizations can play a role in setting standards and guidelines for fair and transparent electoral processes.

Ultimately, the responsibility to combat media manipulation in elections extends to individual citizens. By approaching information with skepticism, verifying sources, and engaging in informed discussions, voters can contribute to a more resilient democratic process. Civic engagement and participation in democratic institutions are crucial for maintaining the integrity of elections and ensuring that the will of the people is accurately represented.

Public Trust in Media A Declining Trend

Public trust in media has been on a downward trajectory, a trend that poses significant implications for society. This decline is not a sudden phenomenon but rather the result of a confluence of factors that have eroded confidence in traditional and digital media alike. Understanding the reasons behind this decline and its consequences is crucial for addressing the challenges it presents.

One of the primary drivers of declining trust in media is the perception of bias. Many consumers believe that media outlets are aligned with specific political or ideological agendas, leading to skewed reporting. This perception is often fueled by the polarization of media landscapes, where outlets cater to niche audiences with content that reinforces existing beliefs. As a result, consumers may feel that they are not receiving a balanced view of events, leading to skepticism and distrust.

The rise of digital media has further complicated the landscape of trust. The sheer volume of information available online can be overwhelming, making it difficult for consumers to discern credible sources from unreliable ones. Social media platforms, in particular, have become breeding grounds for misinformation and sensationalism. The algorithms that govern these platforms often prioritize engagement over accuracy, amplifying content that is emotionally charged or controversial. This can lead to the spread of false information, further eroding trust in media.

The financial pressures faced by media organizations also contribute to the decline in trust. As traditional revenue streams, such as print advertising, have dwindled, many outlets have turned to alternative models, including paywalls and sponsored content. While these strategies can provide much-needed revenue, they can also blur the lines between editorial content and advertising, leading to perceptions of compromised integrity. Consumers may question whether the information they receive is influenced by financial interests, further diminishing trust.

High-profile incidents of journalistic malpractice have also played a role in eroding public confidence. Instances of fabricated stories, plagiarism, or unethical reporting practices can have a lasting impact on the credibility of media organizations. Even when such incidents are isolated, they can contribute to a broader narrative of media unreliability, reinforcing skepticism among consumers.

The decline in trust is not limited to traditional media; it extends to digital platforms and social media influencers as well. As more individuals turn to social media for news and information, the role of influencers and citizen journalists has grown. While these voices can provide valuable perspectives, they often lack the rigorous editorial standards and fact-checking processes of established media organizations. This can lead to the dissemination of inaccurate or biased information, further complicating the landscape of trust.

The consequences of declining trust in media are far-reaching. When consumers lose confidence in the information they receive, it can lead to disengagement from important societal issues. Misinformation can spread unchecked, influencing public opinion and decision-making. In extreme cases, a lack of trust in media can contribute to the erosion of democratic institutions, as citizens become skeptical of the information needed to make informed choices.

Addressing the decline in public trust requires a multifaceted approach. Media organizations must prioritize transparency and accountability in their reporting practices. This includes clearly distinguishing between news and opinion, disclosing potential conflicts of interest, and correcting errors promptly. By demonstrating a commitment to integrity, media outlets can begin to rebuild trust with their audiences.

Media literacy education is another critical component in addressing the trust deficit. By equipping consumers with the skills to critically evaluate information, society can foster a more discerning audience. Media literacy programs can teach individuals how to identify credible sources, recognize bias, and verify information before sharing it. These skills are essential in navigating the complex media landscape and making informed decisions.

Collaboration between media organizations and technology platforms is also essential in combating misinformation and restoring trust. Social media companies can play a role by implementing measures to identify and reduce the spread of false information. This includes partnerships with fact-checking organizations, the use of warning labels, and the promotion of credible sources. By working together, media and technology companies can create a more trustworthy information ecosystem.

The Role of Media in Shaping Political Opinions

Media plays a pivotal role in shaping political opinions, acting as both a mirror and a molder of public perception. Its influence extends across various platforms, from traditional newspapers and television broadcasts to the ever-expanding realm of digital media. Understanding how media shapes political opinions requires an exploration of its mechanisms, its impact on individuals and society, and the responsibilities it bears in a democratic context.

At the heart of media's influence is its ability to set the agenda. By choosing which stories to highlight and how to present them, media outlets can prioritize certain issues over others, effectively guiding public discourse. This agenda-setting function is not merely about what is reported but also about what is omitted. When media consistently covers specific topics, such as economic policies or social justice issues, it signals to the audience that these matters are of paramount importance. Conversely, the absence of coverage on other topics can lead to their marginalization in public consciousness.

Framing is another powerful tool through which media shapes political opinions. The way a story is presented—its language, tone, and context—can significantly influence how it is perceived. For instance, describing a protest as a "peaceful demonstration" versus a "riot" can evoke vastly different reactions from the audience. By framing stories in particular ways, media can sway public sentiment, either reinforcing existing beliefs or challenging them. This framing effect is particularly potent in political reporting, where nuanced language can subtly shape perceptions of candidates, policies, and events.

The rise of digital media has amplified the media's role in shaping political opinions. Social media platforms, in particular, have become influential arenas for political discourse. They offer a space where information spreads rapidly, often without the traditional gatekeeping mechanisms of editorial oversight. This democratization of information has both positive and negative implications. On one hand, it allows for diverse voices and perspectives to be heard, fostering a more inclusive dialogue. On the other hand, it can lead to the proliferation of misinformation and echo chambers, where individuals are exposed only to viewpoints that reinforce their existing beliefs.

The personalization of news through algorithms further complicates the media's role in shaping political opinions. These algorithms curate content based on user preferences and behaviors, creating a tailored news experience. While this personalization can enhance user engagement, it also risks narrowing the scope of information to which individuals are exposed. This phenomenon, often referred to as the "filter bubble," can limit exposure to diverse perspectives, reinforcing polarization and entrenching political divides.

Media's influence on political opinions is not limited to shaping perceptions of issues and events; it also extends to the portrayal of political figures. The way politicians are covered in the media can significantly impact their public image and electoral prospects. Positive coverage can bolster a politician's reputation, while negative reporting can damage it. This dynamic underscores the power of media narratives in shaping political fortunes, as well as the strategic efforts by political actors to manage their media presence.

The interplay between media and politics is further complicated by the phenomenon of media bias. While objectivity is a foundational principle of journalism, complete neutrality is challenging to achieve. Media outlets may exhibit bias, whether intentional or unintentional, in their reporting. This bias can stem from various factors, including ownership interests, editorial policies, and the personal beliefs of journalists. When audiences perceive bias, it can erode trust in media and contribute to skepticism about the information presented.

Despite these challenges, media has a crucial role to play in a democratic society. It serves as a watchdog, holding power to account and providing citizens with the information they need to make informed decisions. This role is particularly important during election cycles, when media coverage can influence voter perceptions and behavior. By scrutinizing candidates, policies, and political processes, media can contribute to a more transparent and accountable political system.

To fulfill its role effectively, media must adhere to principles of accuracy, fairness, and balance. Journalists have a responsibility to verify information, provide context, and present multiple perspectives. This commitment to ethical journalism is essential in maintaining credibility and fostering public trust. Media literacy education is also vital in empowering individuals to critically evaluate the information they consume. By developing skills to discern credible sources, recognize bias, and engage with diverse viewpoints, citizens can become more informed and active participants in the democratic process.

Case Studies Media Manipulation in Recent Elections

In the intricate dance of modern democracy, media manipulation has emerged as a formidable player, capable of swaying public opinion and influencing electoral outcomes. Recent elections across the globe have provided fertile ground for examining how media manipulation operates, revealing both the subtle and overt tactics employed to shape political narratives. By delving into specific case studies, we can uncover the mechanisms of media manipulation and its profound impact on democratic processes.

One of the most scrutinized examples of media manipulation in recent elections occurred during the

2016 United States presidential race. This election highlighted the pervasive influence of misinformation and the strategic use of social media platforms to disseminate false narratives. Various actors, both domestic and foreign, exploited the reach and speed of digital media to spread misleading information, often targeting specific voter demographics. The infamous case of Russian interference, as detailed in numerous investigations, demonstrated how fake news and divisive content were strategically deployed to exacerbate political polarization and undermine trust in democratic institutions.

The tactics used in this election were multifaceted. Social media platforms became breeding grounds for bots and trolls, automated accounts designed to amplify certain messages and create the illusion of widespread support or opposition. These bots were adept at mimicking human behavior, engaging with real users, and spreading disinformation at an unprecedented scale. The result was an environment where truth and falsehoods were often indistinguishable, leaving voters vulnerable to manipulation.

Another significant case study can be found in the 2018 Brazilian presidential election, where media manipulation played a crucial role in shaping the political landscape. The election saw the rise of Jair Bolsonaro, a candidate who effectively harnessed social media to bypass traditional media channels and connect directly with voters. Bolsonaro's campaign capitalized on the viral nature of WhatsApp, a messaging platform widely used in Brazil, to disseminate targeted messages and misinformation.

This approach allowed the campaign to reach millions of voters with minimal oversight, spreading content that ranged from exaggerated claims to outright falsehoods.

The use of WhatsApp in this context exemplifies how media manipulation can exploit private communication channels, making it difficult to track and counteract false information. Unlike public social media platforms, messaging apps offer a degree of privacy and intimacy that can enhance the credibility of shared content. This dynamic poses significant challenges for fact-checkers and regulators, who struggle to monitor and address misinformation circulating in closed networks.

In the United Kingdom, the 2016 Brexit referendum serves as another illustrative case of media manipulation's impact on electoral outcomes. The referendum campaign was marked by a deluge of misleading claims and sensationalist headlines, often propagated by tabloid newspapers and online platforms. One of the most notorious examples was the claim that leaving the European Union would free up £350 million a week for the National Health Service, a figure that was widely debunked but nonetheless gained traction among voters.

The Brexit campaign also saw the strategic use of targeted advertising on social media, leveraging data analytics to identify and influence swing voters. This approach, often referred to as microtargeting, involves tailoring messages to specific audiences based on their online behavior and preferences. By delivering personalized content, campaigns can effectively manipulate perceptions and sway opinions, often without the knowledge of the broader public.

These case studies underscore the evolving nature of media manipulation in the digital age. Traditional media outlets, once the primary gatekeepers of information, now share the stage with a myriad of digital platforms that offer both opportunities and challenges for democratic engagement. The decentralization of information has democratized access to news, but it has also created fertile ground for manipulation, where false narratives can spread rapidly and with little accountability.

Addressing media manipulation requires a multifaceted approach that involves not only technological solutions but also regulatory frameworks and public awareness. Social media companies have a responsibility to implement measures that curb the spread of misinformation, such as improving content moderation and transparency in advertising. However, these efforts must be balanced with the protection of free speech and privacy rights, ensuring that measures do not inadvertently stifle legitimate discourse.

Regulators and policymakers also play a crucial role in combating media manipulation. By enacting legislation that promotes transparency in political advertising and holds platforms accountable for the content they host, governments can help safeguard the integrity of electoral processes. Additionally, international cooperation is essential in addressing cross-border manipulation efforts, as digital platforms often operate beyond the jurisdiction of any single nation.

Public awareness and media literacy are equally vital in countering media manipulation. Educating citizens about the tactics used to manipulate information and encouraging critical thinking can empower individuals to discern credible sources from falsehoods. Media literacy programs should be integrated into educational curricula, equipping future generations with the skills needed to navigate an increasingly complex information landscape.

Strategies for Protecting Democratic Institutions

Safeguarding democratic institutions is a task of paramount importance in an era where these structures face unprecedented challenges. The resilience of democracy hinges on the ability to adapt and fortify against threats that range from external interference to internal erosion. To protect these institutions, a multifaceted approach is essential, encompassing legal, technological, and societal strategies that work in concert to uphold the principles of democracy.

One of the foundational strategies for protecting democratic institutions is the reinforcement of legal frameworks. Robust legal systems serve as the backbone of democracy, ensuring that the rule of law prevails and that institutions operate within a defined set of principles. This involves enacting and enforcing laws that promote transparency, accountability, and fairness in governance. Anti-corruption measures, for instance, are crucial in preventing the misuse of power and resources, which can undermine public trust and the integrity of democratic institutions.

Judicial independence is another critical component of a strong legal framework. Courts must remain impartial and free from political influence to effectively uphold the law and protect citizens' rights. Ensuring that judges are appointed based on merit rather than political allegiance can help maintain the judiciary's credibility and authority. Additionally, mechanisms for judicial review and oversight can provide checks and balances on other branches of government, preventing the concentration of power and potential abuses.

Technological advancements present both opportunities and challenges for democratic institutions. On one hand, technology can enhance transparency and citizen engagement by providing platforms for open communication and information sharing. E-governance initiatives, for example, can streamline public services and make government operations more accessible and accountable to citizens. On the other hand, the digital landscape also poses risks, such as cyberattacks and the spread of misinformation, which can destabilize democratic processes.

To mitigate these risks, investing in cybersecurity is paramount. Protecting critical infrastructure, such as electoral systems and government databases, from cyber threats is essential to maintaining the integrity of democratic institutions. This requires collaboration between government agencies, private sector partners, and international allies to develop and implement robust cybersecurity measures. Regular audits, threat assessments, and incident response plans can help identify vulnerabilities and ensure that systems are resilient against attacks.

Addressing the challenge of misinformation requires a comprehensive approach that involves both technological solutions and public education. Social media platforms and online news outlets must take responsibility for curbing the spread of false information by implementing effective content moderation policies and promoting credible sources. At the same time, fostering media literacy among citizens is crucial in empowering individuals to critically evaluate the information they encounter. Educational programs that teach critical thinking and digital literacy skills can help citizens discern fact from fiction and make informed decisions.

Public participation and civic engagement are vital components of a healthy democracy. Encouraging active citizen involvement in the political process can strengthen democratic institutions by ensuring that they remain responsive to the needs and aspirations of the populace. This can be achieved through initiatives that promote voter registration and turnout, as well as efforts to engage marginalized communities that may feel disenfranchised or excluded from the political process.

Creating spaces for dialogue and deliberation can also enhance civic engagement. Town hall meetings, public forums, and online platforms for discussion provide opportunities for citizens to voice their opinions, share ideas, and collaborate on solutions to common challenges. By fostering a culture of open dialogue and mutual respect, democratic institutions can build trust and legitimacy among the public.

Education plays a pivotal role in nurturing democratic values and preparing future generations to uphold and protect democratic institutions. Civic education programs that emphasize the importance of democratic principles, such as equality, justice, and freedom, can instill a sense of responsibility and commitment to the common good. Schools and universities can serve as incubators for democratic engagement by encouraging students to participate in debates, simulations, and community service projects that promote active citizenship.

International cooperation is another key strategy for protecting democratic institutions. Democracies around the world face similar challenges, and collaboration can provide valuable opportunities for sharing best practices, resources, and expertise. Multilateral organizations and alliances can facilitate dialogue and cooperation on issues such as election security, human rights, and the rule of law. By working together, democracies can present a united front against threats to democratic governance and promote stability and peace on a global scale.

The role of civil society organizations in protecting democratic institutions cannot be overstated. These organizations serve as watchdogs, advocates, and educators, holding governments accountable and promoting transparency and inclusivity. Supporting the work of civil society groups through funding, capacity-building, and legal protections can enhance their ability to contribute to democratic resilience. By fostering partnerships between government and civil society, democratic institutions can benefit from diverse perspectives and expertise.

Chapter 6

Global Perspectives on Media Manipulation

Media Manipulation in Authoritarian Regimes

In the shadowy corridors of authoritarian regimes, media manipulation emerges as a potent tool wielded to maintain control and suppress dissent. These regimes, often characterized by their centralized power and lack of democratic freedoms, understand the immense influence of media in shaping public perception and opinion. By controlling the narrative, they can effectively stifle opposition, legitimize their rule, and perpetuate their ideologies. The strategies employed in this manipulation are as varied as they are insidious, ranging from censorship and propaganda to the co-opting of digital platforms.

Censorship stands as a cornerstone of media manipulation in authoritarian regimes. By restricting access to information, these governments can prevent the dissemination of ideas that challenge their authority. This often involves the suppression of independent journalism, where media outlets are either state-owned or heavily regulated to ensure compliance with government narratives. Journalists who dare to report on sensitive issues or criticize the regime face harassment, imprisonment, or worse. The chilling effect of such measures stifles free expression and creates an environment where self-censorship becomes a survival tactic for those in the media industry.

Propaganda is another powerful weapon in the arsenal of authoritarian regimes. Through carefully crafted messages, these governments seek to shape public perception and reinforce their legitimacy. State-controlled media outlets churn out content that glorifies the regime's achievements while demonizing its opponents. Historical revisionism is often employed to rewrite the past in a manner that bolsters the regime's narrative, casting it as the savior of the nation. This manipulation of information serves to create a distorted reality where the regime's actions are justified, and dissent is portrayed as treasonous.

The advent of digital technology has introduced new dimensions to media manipulation. Authoritarian regimes have adapted to the digital age by exploiting social media and online platforms to further their agendas. These platforms, initially seen as tools for democratization and free expression, have become battlegrounds for information warfare. Regimes deploy armies of bots and trolls to spread disinformation, amplify pro-government messages, and drown out dissenting voices. By flooding the digital space with noise, they can obscure the truth and create confusion among the populace.

Surveillance and data collection are also integral to the manipulation of media in authoritarian regimes. By monitoring online activities, these governments can identify and target individuals who pose a threat to their control. This surveillance extends to social media, where users' posts and interactions are scrutinized for signs of dissent. The fear of being watched creates a climate of paranoia, discouraging citizens from expressing their true opinions and further entrenching the regime's hold on power.

Education and media literacy play a crucial role in countering media manipulation. By equipping citizens with the skills to critically analyze information, societies can build resilience against the distortions propagated by authoritarian regimes. Educational initiatives that promote critical thinking and digital literacy can empower individuals to discern fact from fiction and recognize propaganda when they encounter it. This awareness is essential in fostering a culture of skepticism and inquiry, where citizens are less susceptible to manipulation.

International cooperation and advocacy are also vital in addressing media manipulation in authoritarian regimes. Global organizations and democratic governments can exert pressure on these regimes to uphold freedom of expression and protect journalists. By supporting independent media outlets and providing platforms for dissenting voices, the international community can help counter the narratives imposed by authoritarian governments. Sanctions and diplomatic measures can also be employed to hold regimes accountable for their actions and encourage reforms.

The role of technology companies in combating media manipulation cannot be overlooked. As gatekeepers of digital platforms, these companies have a responsibility to ensure that their services are not exploited for nefarious purposes. Implementing robust content moderation policies and algorithms that detect and remove disinformation can help mitigate the impact of media manipulation. Transparency in data collection and user privacy protections are also essential in safeguarding against surveillance and ensuring that digital spaces remain open and free.

Grassroots movements and civil society organizations play a pivotal role in resisting media manipulation. By mobilizing communities and raising awareness, these groups can challenge the narratives imposed by authoritarian regimes and advocate for change. Citizen journalism and alternative media outlets provide platforms for voices that are often marginalized or silenced, offering diverse perspectives and countering the homogeneity of state-controlled media. Through collective action and solidarity, civil society can create a groundswell of resistance that challenges the status quo and demands accountability.

Comparative Analysis Media Freedom Across Countries

Media freedom varies significantly across the globe, reflecting the diverse political, cultural, and economic landscapes of different countries. This comparative analysis seeks to illuminate the factors that contribute to these variations, offering insights into the complex interplay between media and governance. By examining specific examples, we can better understand how media freedom is both a reflection of and a catalyst for broader societal dynamics.

In democratic nations, media freedom is often enshrined in law, serving as a cornerstone of open societies. These countries typically boast a vibrant press landscape, where journalists operate with relative autonomy and are protected by legal frameworks that uphold freedom of expression. For instance, in countries like Norway and Finland, media freedom is not only a constitutional right but also a cultural norm. These nations consistently rank high on global press freedom indices, thanks to their commitment to transparency, accountability, and the protection of journalistic integrity. The media in these countries plays a crucial role in holding power to account, fostering informed citizenry, and facilitating public discourse.

Conversely, in authoritarian regimes, media freedom is often severely restricted. Governments in these countries view the press as a potential threat to their authority and employ various tactics to control and manipulate information. In places like North Korea and Eritrea, the state maintains a tight grip on media outlets, ensuring that only government-approved narratives reach the public. Independent journalism is virtually non-existent, and dissenting voices are swiftly silenced through censorship, intimidation, or imprisonment. The lack of media freedom in these regimes stifles public debate, limits access to information, and perpetuates a cycle of oppression and misinformation.

Between these two extremes lie countries with varying degrees of media freedom, often influenced by their unique historical, political, and social contexts. In nations undergoing political transitions, such as

Myanmar or Sudan, media freedom can be in a state of flux. These countries may experience periods of relative openness, where independent media flourishes and journalists can report on sensitive issues without fear of retribution. However, such freedoms are often precarious, subject to the whims of political leaders or shifting power dynamics. The struggle for media freedom in these contexts is emblematic of broader democratic aspirations and the challenges of navigating complex political landscapes.

Economic factors also play a significant role in shaping media freedom. In some countries, media outlets are heavily reliant on government funding or advertising revenue from state-owned enterprises, which can compromise their independence. This is particularly evident in nations with weak economies or limited private sector development, where financial pressures can lead to self-censorship or biased reporting. Conversely, in countries with robust economies and diverse media markets, outlets may have greater financial autonomy, allowing them to pursue investigative journalism and hold power to account without fear of economic repercussions.

Cultural attitudes towards media and journalism further influence the degree of media freedom in different countries. In societies where the press is viewed as a vital component of democracy, there is often greater public support for media independence and protection of journalists. This cultural endorsement can serve as a bulwark against attempts to curtail media freedom, empowering journalists to pursue their work with confidence. In contrast, in cultures where the media is perceived as an extension of political power or a tool for propaganda, there may be less public outcry against restrictions on press freedom, allowing governments to exert greater control over the media landscape.

Technological advancements have introduced new dimensions to media freedom, both enhancing and complicating the landscape. The rise of digital media and social platforms has democratized information dissemination, enabling citizen journalism and alternative voices to flourish. In countries with limited traditional media freedom, these digital spaces can serve as vital outlets for dissent and independent reporting. However, they also present challenges, as governments increasingly employ sophisticated surveillance and censorship technologies to monitor and control online content. The digital realm thus becomes a contested space, where the battle for media freedom is fought on new fronts.

International organizations and advocacy groups play a crucial role in promoting media freedom across countries. By monitoring press freedom violations, providing support to journalists, and advocating for policy changes, these entities help to hold governments accountable and foster environments conducive to free expression. Global indices and reports, such as those published by Reporters Without Borders or the Committee to Protect Journalists, offer valuable insights into the state of media freedom worldwide, highlighting areas of concern and progress.

The comparative analysis of media freedom across countries underscores the importance of context in understanding the dynamics at play. While legal frameworks and political systems are critical determinants, cultural, economic, and technological factors also shape the media landscape in profound ways. By recognizing these complexities, we can better appreciate the challenges and opportunities for advancing media freedom globally.

The Role of International Organizations in Media Regulation

International organizations play a pivotal role in shaping the landscape of media regulation across the globe. These entities, ranging from intergovernmental bodies to non-governmental organizations, exert influence through policy development, advocacy, and capacity-building initiatives. Their involvement is crucial in promoting media freedom, ensuring ethical standards, and fostering a diverse and pluralistic media environment. By examining the multifaceted contributions of these organizations, we can gain a deeper understanding of their impact on media regulation and the challenges they face in an ever-evolving global context.

One of the primary functions of international organizations in media regulation is the establishment of normative frameworks that guide national policies. These frameworks often emphasize the importance of media freedom, pluralism, and independence as fundamental components of democratic societies. For instance, UNESCO, as a specialized agency of the

United Nations, has been instrumental in promoting the principles of free and independent media through its various declarations and conventions. The Windhoek Declaration, adopted in 1991, is a landmark document that underscores the necessity of a free press for the development and maintenance of democracy. Such frameworks serve as benchmarks for countries to align their media policies with international standards, fostering a more consistent and coherent approach to media regulation worldwide.

In addition to setting normative standards, international organizations engage in advocacy efforts to promote media freedom and protect journalists. Organizations like Reporters Without Borders and the Committee to Protect Journalists play a critical role in monitoring press freedom violations, raising awareness about threats to journalists, and advocating for policy changes at both national and international levels. Their efforts help to hold governments accountable for their actions and create pressure for reforms that enhance media freedom. By shining a spotlight on abuses and mobilizing public opinion, these organizations contribute to a global culture that values and defends the rights of journalists and media outlets.

Capacity-building initiatives are another key area where international organizations contribute to media regulation. By providing training, resources, and technical assistance, these entities help to strengthen the capacity of media professionals and regulatory bodies to navigate complex media environments. The International Federation of Journalists, for example, offers training programs that equip journalists with the skills needed to report ethically and safely in challenging contexts. Similarly, the World Association of Newspapers and News Publishers provides support to media outlets in developing countries, helping them to build sustainable business models and improve their editorial standards. Through these initiatives, international organizations empower media actors to operate more effectively and responsibly, contributing to a more robust and resilient media landscape.

The role of international organizations in media regulation also extends to fostering dialogue and cooperation among stakeholders. By convening forums, conferences, and workshops, these entities create platforms for the exchange of ideas, experiences, and best practices. Such gatherings facilitate collaboration between governments, media professionals, civil society, and academia, enabling them to address common challenges and explore innovative solutions. The Global Forum for Media Development, for instance, brings together media development organizations from around the world to share insights and coordinate efforts to support independent media. By promoting dialogue and cooperation, international organizations help to build networks of solidarity and mutual support that strengthen the global media ecosystem.

Despite their significant contributions, international organizations face numerous challenges in their efforts to influence media regulation. One of the primary obstacles is the diversity of political, cultural, and economic contexts in which they operate. Media regulation is inherently shaped by national circumstances, and what works in one country may not be applicable in another. This diversity requires international organizations to adopt flexible and context-sensitive approaches that respect local realities while promoting universal principles. Balancing these considerations can be complex, requiring a nuanced understanding of the interplay between global norms and local practices.

Another challenge is the growing complexity of the media landscape, driven by rapid technological advancements and the proliferation of digital platforms. The rise of social media, online news outlets, and citizen journalism has transformed the way information is produced, distributed, and consumed. This shift presents both opportunities and challenges for media regulation, as traditional regulatory frameworks may struggle to keep pace with the dynamic nature of digital media. International organizations must adapt their strategies to address issues such as misinformation, digital privacy, and platform accountability, while continuing to uphold the principles of media freedom and pluralism.

The political climate in which international organizations operate can also pose challenges to their efforts in media regulation. In some countries, governments may view international involvement in media affairs as an infringement on their sovereignty or as a threat to their control over information. This resistance can hinder the implementation of international standards and limit the effectiveness of advocacy and capacity-building initiatives. To navigate these challenges, international organizations must engage in diplomatic efforts to build trust and foster constructive relationships with national authorities, emphasizing the mutual benefits of media freedom and regulation.

Cultural Differences in Media Consumption and Perception

Media consumption and perception are deeply intertwined with cultural contexts, shaping how individuals interpret and engage with content. These cultural differences manifest in various ways, influencing preferences, interpretations, and the overall impact of media on audiences. Understanding these nuances is essential for media creators, marketers, and policymakers aiming to reach diverse audiences effectively.

Cultural values and norms play a significant role in determining media preferences. In collectivist societies, where community and family are prioritized, media content often reflects themes of unity, harmony, and social responsibility. For instance, in many Asian countries, television dramas and films frequently emphasize family bonds and societal obligations. Conversely, in individualistic cultures, such as those in the United States and Western Europe, media often highlights personal achievement, independence, and self-expression. These cultural orientations shape the types of narratives and characters that resonate with audiences, influencing their media consumption choices.

Language is another critical factor in media perception. It serves as a vehicle for conveying cultural nuances, humor, and emotion. Multilingual societies, like India and Switzerland, present unique challenges and opportunities for media producers. Content must be tailored to accommodate linguistic diversity, ensuring that it resonates with different language groups. Subtitles, dubbing, and localization are common strategies employed to bridge language barriers, but they can also alter the original meaning and cultural context of the content. This linguistic adaptation requires careful consideration to maintain authenticity and cultural relevance.

Cultural differences also affect the interpretation of media messages. Symbolism, humor, and non-verbal cues can vary significantly across cultures, leading to diverse interpretations of the same content. For example, humor that relies on sarcasm or irony may be well-received in some Western cultures but misunderstood or deemed inappropriate in others. Similarly, gestures and body language that convey specific meanings in one culture may hold entirely different connotations elsewhere. Media creators must be mindful of these cultural variations to avoid miscommunication and ensure that their messages are accurately conveyed.

The role of media in shaping cultural identity and values cannot be overstated. Media serves as a mirror, reflecting societal norms and values, while also acting as a catalyst for change. In many cultures, media has been instrumental in challenging traditional norms and promoting progressive values. For instance, the portrayal of gender roles in media has evolved significantly over the years, influencing societal perceptions and expectations. In some cultures, media has played a pivotal role in advancing gender equality by showcasing strong, independent female characters and challenging stereotypes. However, this influence is not uniform across cultures, as deeply ingrained cultural norms can resist change, leading to varying degrees of acceptance and adaptation.

Globalization has further complicated the landscape of media consumption and perception. The proliferation of digital platforms and the internet has facilitated the cross-cultural exchange of media content, exposing audiences to diverse perspectives and narratives. While this has led to greater cultural understanding and appreciation, it has also raised concerns about cultural homogenization and the erosion of local identities. The dominance of Western media, in particular, has sparked debates about cultural imperialism and the need to preserve indigenous cultures and languages. Balancing the benefits of global media exposure with the preservation of cultural heritage remains a complex challenge for policymakers and media producers alike.

The impact of cultural differences on media consumption extends to advertising and marketing strategies. Brands seeking to expand their reach across borders must navigate the intricacies of cultural preferences and sensitivities. Successful global marketing campaigns often involve a deep understanding of local cultures, allowing brands to tailor their messages and products to resonate with diverse audiences. This cultural adaptation can involve modifying product features, packaging, and advertising content to align with local tastes and values. However, missteps in cultural sensitivity can lead to backlash and damage to a brand's reputation, underscoring the importance of cultural competence in global marketing efforts.

Social media platforms have emerged as powerful tools for cross-cultural communication and engagement. They provide a space for individuals to share their cultural experiences, connect with others, and participate in global conversations. However, cultural differences can also lead to misunderstandings and conflicts in online interactions. The anonymity and immediacy of social media can exacerbate these issues, as users may be less mindful of cultural sensitivities and more prone to expressing controversial or offensive opinions. Promoting cultural awareness and empathy in online spaces is essential to fostering positive cross-cultural interactions and reducing the potential for conflict.

Media literacy is a crucial skill in navigating the complexities of cultural differences in media consumption and perception. It empowers individuals to critically analyze media content, recognize cultural biases, and appreciate diverse perspectives. Media literacy education can help audiences become more discerning consumers of media, enabling them to identify and challenge stereotypes, misinformation, and cultural assumptions. By fostering media literacy, educators and policymakers can equip individuals with the tools needed to engage with media content thoughtfully and responsibly, promoting a more inclusive and informed media landscape.

Global Efforts to Combat Media Manipulation

Media manipulation is a pervasive issue that transcends borders, affecting societies worldwide. As the digital age continues to evolve, so too do the tactics and strategies employed by those seeking to distort information for various purposes. Recognizing the profound impact of media manipulation on public perception, trust, and democracy, global efforts have been mobilized to combat this challenge. These initiatives encompass a range of strategies, from policy development and technological innovation to education and cross-border collaboration.

Governments around the world have taken significant steps to address media manipulation through legislative measures. Many countries have enacted laws aimed at curbing the spread of misinformation and disinformation, particularly on social media platforms. These laws often require platforms to remove false content swiftly and impose penalties for non-compliance. However, the implementation of such regulations is not without controversy. Critics argue that overly stringent laws may infringe on freedom of speech and lead to censorship. Balancing the need to protect the public from harmful content while preserving fundamental rights remains a delicate task for policymakers.

International organizations have also played a crucial role in combating media manipulation. The United Nations, for instance, has launched initiatives to promote media literacy and support independent journalism. By fostering an informed and discerning public, these efforts aim to reduce the susceptibility of individuals to manipulated content. Additionally, the European Union has been at the forefront of developing comprehensive strategies to tackle disinformation. The EU's Code of Practice on Disinformation, a voluntary framework for online platforms, advertisers, and other stakeholders, seeks to enhance transparency, promote credible information, and empower users to make informed decisions.

Technological advancements have provided both challenges and solutions in the fight against media manipulation. On one hand, the rise of deepfake technology and sophisticated algorithms has made it easier to create and disseminate false information. On the other hand, technology has also equipped researchers and developers with tools to detect and counteract manipulated content. Artificial intelligence and machine learning algorithms are increasingly being used to identify patterns of misinformation and flag suspicious content. These technologies, while promising, require continuous refinement to keep pace with the evolving tactics of manipulators.

Collaboration between governments, tech companies, and civil society is essential in addressing the multifaceted nature of media manipulation. Public-private partnerships have emerged as a powerful mechanism for pooling resources and expertise. For example, tech giants like Google, Facebook, and Twitter have partnered with fact-checking organizations to verify information and reduce the spread of false content on their platforms. These collaborations often involve sharing data, developing best practices, and coordinating responses to emerging threats. However, the effectiveness of these partnerships depends on the willingness of all parties to engage transparently and prioritize the public interest.

Education and media literacy are fundamental components of global efforts to combat media manipulation. By equipping individuals with the skills to critically evaluate information, societies can build resilience against misinformation. Educational programs aimed at enhancing media literacy are being implemented in schools, universities, and communities worldwide. These programs often focus on teaching individuals how to identify credible sources, recognize biased or misleading content, and understand the motivations behind media manipulation. Empowering individuals with these skills not only helps them navigate the complex media landscape but also fosters a culture of critical thinking and informed decision-making.

The role of independent journalism in countering media manipulation cannot be overstated. Journalists serve as watchdogs, holding power to account and providing the public with accurate and reliable information. Supporting independent media outlets, particularly in regions where press freedom is under threat, is crucial in maintaining a diverse and pluralistic media environment. International organizations and non-governmental organizations often provide funding, training, and resources to bolster the capacity of independent journalists. By strengthening the foundations of journalism, these efforts contribute to a more transparent and accountable media ecosystem.

Cross-border collaboration is vital in addressing the global nature of media manipulation. Disinformation campaigns often transcend national boundaries, necessitating coordinated responses from multiple countries. International coalitions and alliances have been formed to share intelligence, develop joint strategies, and conduct research on media manipulation tactics. These collaborations enable countries to learn from each other's experiences, leverage collective expertise, and enhance their ability to respond to emerging threats. However, geopolitical tensions and differing national interests can pose challenges to effective collaboration, highlighting the need for diplomacy and mutual understanding.